Heavenly Impact
Symbolic Praise, Worship, and Intercession
"On Earth as it is in Heaven"

From Genesis to Revelation, we see a definite pattern of worship, ordained by God, ancient yet eternal. This book presents a clear and concise picture, based upon scripture that reveals the major significance that is felt in the heavenly realm when symbolic tools are used during times of praise, worship and intercession on this earthly plane.

Worship and praise were never meant to be passive. We see that Old and New Testament Christians who were pursuing God were aggressive in symbolic praise and worship. They were completely surrendered to the will of God for their lives, no matter what the circumstances looked like. The worse the circumstances, the more aggressive in praise they were!
When the Hebrew children praised with these symbolic instruments the presence of the Lord filled their physical surroundings. They used some of these instruments as a point of contact intercession tool in the face of their enemies. They were directed by the Lord to do this. They understood the reason for their victory in battle was due to their humble dependence on the Lord, not upon their skill. As they moved in faith the Lord and His hosts showed up, fought and won their battles for them.

My prayer is that as you read this book, your heart will be stirred and your spirit will be freed from fleshly limitations that you may have placed upon it. You will be assured that the Lord not only approves of this pro-active style of worship, but also fully, endorses it, after all - He created it. If you have never praised or worshipped in this type of visually expressive style, it is possible you will make a transition from being a reserved and possibly skeptical spectator to an active participator.

Foreword

This book is long overdue. The Body of Christ needs much understanding concerning the adornments of God. God wants to express Himself through the beauty of His creation and I believe this book will give insight into this area of ministry.

When I first met Jeanette the Lord gave me the following prophecy for her: (At that time I did not know that she was involved with making symbolic Tabrets), "I see you signing books." God is saying; "You will be writing books based on your experiences combined with scriptures." I see you dancing with flags, streamers and tabrets. The books will have to do with praise, worship and intercession. These books will be anointed by God and will be read all over the world. "
May 1998.   Aimee Kovacs.

Aimee Kovacs, Ph.D. is the author of the best selling book *DANCING INTO THE ANOINTING*, which is used in churches around the world as a textbook on praise and worship.

We regret to announce that at the time of the publishing of this book Aimee received an unexpected divine promotion and went home to heaven to be with the Lord. She was greatly loved and admired for her inexhaustible spiritual strength and passion to reach unreached people with the gospel of Jesus Christ. She was responsible for spiritual oversight of 82 churches around the world. She traveled extensively preaching, prophesying and ministering to those in need. Aimee was a wonderful friend whom I will greatly miss. I consider it a great honor and privilege that she wrote the forward to *Heavenly Impact*, and wish to include it as a memorial to her and the Lord for the prophetic word that she gave to me concerning this book coming to fruition.

Table of Contents

Chapter 1
Symbolic Praise, Worship and Intercession

Symbolism is a language created by God, a universal means of communication that extends beyond the boundaries of words. The word symbolic is defined by Webster's Encyclopedic Dictionary as an object used to represent something abstract. (The dove as a peace symbol). An emblem used to express or represent something else. My definition would be; Symbolic praise, worship and intercession is "the use or the exhibiting of a symbol as a point of contact to express the invisible by means of a visible representation" (the use of one thing to represent another.)

This is a visual, dramatic, and expressive style of worship when combined with Holy Spirit led movement, which releases our faith in a physical manner. The Holy Spirit is stirring our hearts to get up and get moving. If the Lord can get us to move beyond our own flesh, which is usually self-conscious, it will be easier for Him to use us in the supernatural arena.

We are instructed to move by faith and not by sight. Moving in the symbolic prophetic is a faith walk. As we are obedient to the Lord's instruction, combining faith with action, we will usher in God's divine purposes. Noah, moving by faith, out of obedience and not by sight, built an ark as God directed him. God might not be telling us to build an ark, but our responsibility is to be obedient to do what He says to do and leave the results in His hands. Some might point out that not all actions performed during praise and worship will come under the heading of prophetic symbolic. Only the Lord knows the impact of our actions, and how He might use them for future purposes. I am sure that the woman in *Matt.26: 12;* had no idea of the magnitude of her simple, symbolic, obedient action.
"For in pouring this fragrant oil on my body, she did it for my burial. Assuredly, I say to you, wherever this gospel is preached in

the whole world, what this woman has done will also be told as a memorial to her." SFLB.

The Lord has given us written, user friendly instructions describing in detail how He wants us, as His children, to praise and worship Him. As we study the Bible we can readily see that the use of worship adornments is a pre-ordained, ancient, yet eternal style of praise and worship blessed by the Lord.

Ps.150: 3-6 "Praise him with the sound of the trumpet; praise him with the psaltry and harp. Praise him with the timbrel and dance; praise him with stringed instruments and organs. Praise him upon the loud cymbals; praise him upon the high-sounding cymbals. Let everyone that hath breath praise the Lord. Praise ye the Lord."

1.Sam. 18:6 "And it came to pass as they came, when David was returned from the slaughter of the Philistine, that the women came out of all the cities of Israel, singing and dancing, to meet King Saul, with tabrets, with joy, and with instruments of music."

We are to go forth in holy joy expressing ourselves in the dance, adorned with our symbolic instruments!
Ps. 20:5 "May we shout for joy when we hear of your victory, flying banners to honor our God." NLT.

Much like the New Testament believers who waved palm branches and laid their garments down on the road, paving the way for the Messiah as He rode into town on the back of a donkey, we are waving our symbolic instruments in anticipation, ushering in the second and last coming of the King of kings and the Lord of lords. *John 12:13.*

Rev. 7:9; "After this I saw a vast crowd, too great to count, from every nation and tribe and people and language, standing in front of the throne and before the Lamb. They were clothed in white and held palm branches in their hands."

2

Symbolic Praise, Worship and Intercession

These symbolic instruments are strictly a point of contact, but a powerful one in the spiritual realm. Most symbolic instruments that are available for our use on this earthly plane represent a divine counterpart in the heavenly realm. Every action performed under the unction of the Holy Spirit during praise, worship, and intercession has a corresponding heavenly reaction to bring about the divine purposes of God.

In most cases the same instrument you are using to praise the Lord with is being used for a dual or two-fold purpose in the heavenly realm, which is to render judgment to our enemies! The same word spelled differently (duel) means a pre-arranged fight between two persons armed with deadly weapons. Do not fear this pre-arranged fight. With the worship comes the warship.

In this scripture, we see that as we praise with the symbolic tabret in our hands, singing scripture there is a corresponding action being performed in heaven by the Lord Himself, with these instruments in His hands. *Isa. 30:32 "And in every place where the grounded staff shall pass (the word of God) which the Lord shall lay upon the Assyrian (enemy), it shall be with tabrets and harps; and in battles of shaking will he fight with it."*

The word shaking in this scripture refers back to its root meaning in the Hebrew/Greek as brandishing in victory. What a joy!

In the following chapters, you will read of examples of symbolic adornments that the Lord instructed the Hebrew children to use. The action of using these instruments will be described and the corresponding reaction that occurred in the heavenlies simultaneously, which caused an impact upon the earth, specifically targeted to the situation.

As we combine faith with action in this physical realm, we bridge the gap between the old covenant prophecies and the end time fulfillment of those prophecies. Symbolic praise, worship and intercession are being launched in an unprecedented way by the

Heavenly Impact

Holy Spirit in preparation for the return of Yeshua (Jesus) the bridegroom coming for His bride.
This is one of the many unique facets of worship ministry that Heavenly Impact explores. I don't intend in any way to dimish the importance or sovereignty of any other worship style, nor am I attempting to establish a doctrine in this area.

Scripture clearly reveals that this is an area that is close and dear to Father God's heart. As we choose to move in faith using the symbolic items He has ordained we will bring joy to His heart and favor upon ourselves. We will provide a strategic piece of the pattern set forth by David, as the Lord restores the Tabernacle of David.

Amos 9:11 "In that day will I raise up the tabernacle of David that is fallen, and close up the breaches thereof; and I will raise up his ruins, and I will build it as in the days of old:"

Chapter 2
The Language of Symbolism

 Through an in-depth examination of scripture we see that Jesus used the vehicle of parables, rich in symbolism to teach practical life lessons that applied not only in the former days, but also in these latter days. Parable: a usually short fictitious story that illustrates a moral attitude or a religious principle. *Merriam-Webster Online Dictionary.* I have heard the definition expressed in this way. At the surface level a parable is an interesting, entertaining story, which uses everyday examples as symbols, with a much deeper spiritual parallel.
Matt. 13:34 "All these things spake Jesus unto the multitude in parables; and without a parable spake he not unto them."

1st. Cor.2:14 "…but the natural man receiveth not the things of the Spirit of God: for they are foolishness unto him: neither can he know them, because they are spiritually discerned."
We can't expect people who don't know the Lord to understand some of our actions of the symbolic nature. Sometimes even those who do love the Lord have a hard time understanding the deeper parallels of spiritual truths, demonstrated thru the vehicle of symbolism.

 As we mature in the Lord by studying His word, we become more familiar with this symbolic language. We see that symbolism was deeply interwoven in almost everything He said or did in His every day life. The Bible and the Holy Spirit will teach us so we can begin to teach as he did, and do those things that we read of Him doing. Our desire should be to pattern ourselves after Jesus. He says that we will do greater things than He did. *John 14:12 "Verily, verily, I say unto you, He that believeth on me, the works that I do shall he do also; and greater works than these shall he do; because I go unto my Father."*

Heavenly Impact

The ministry of Jesus was launched by a symbolic act.

Mark 1:9 "… and it came to pass in those days that Jesus came from Nazareth of Galilee, and was baptized of John in the Jordan. And straightway coming up out of the water, he saw the heavens opened, and the spirit like a dove descending upon him: and there came a voice from heaven, saying, Thou art my beloved Son, in whom I am well pleased."

This act invoked an immediate response of approval from the Father in heaven. Jesus demonstrated an object lesson for our benefit. The spiritual/physical act of burying our old sin nature under the water. This symbolic act was the initiation of a lifestyle of instruction through the words of parables or similitudes acted out by Jesus and His disciples.
The physical life of Jesus coming to an end on this earth was also punctuated by a symbolic act. Dying on the cross for our sins. The Lord gave an immediate response to this act also. The veil in the temple was rent in two. This was a non-verbal symbolic language that stated that we now had access into the Father's presence through the death of His son.

This language of symbolism is a soundless language, which is heard across the expanse of the heavenlies loud and clear!

In this day the Holy Spirit is moving upon the face of the earth restoring the Tabernacle of David.
Acts 15:16 "After this I will return, and will build again the tabernacle of David which is fallen down; and I will build again the ruins thereof, and I will set it up: That the residue of men might seek after the Lord, and all the Gentiles, upon whom My name is called, saith the Lord, who doeth all these things."

The Language of Symbolism

The Tabernacle of David was not a permanent structure such as a building. The term is symbolic for each believer being a Tabernacle of praise unto the Lord. We are to be the worship and praise in the earth unto the Most High God. If we aren't, the rocks will cry out. He is adorning His tabernacles-us with symbolic expressive instruments of adornment. *Is.61:10.*
These instruments include tabrets, tambourines, flags, streamers, banners, shofars, mat-tehs', billows, veils and more. As David created instruments led of the Holy Spirit to be used in the worship of the Most High God, so shall we.

<u>Like the movements of a dance, each symbolic worship tool has definition and is an expression of faith language in the heavenly realm.</u>

The symbolic prophetic is an eternal relevant type of ministry! What may have been considered unchartered territory is fast becoming the land of living symbolic praise. A dancer studies to learn a vocabulary of movement; we can do the same with symbolic items.
There will be different forms of creative expression according to individual gifting and preferences of style, which can communicate the same message. In this visual artisan ministry there may be times when you will be led of the Holy Spirit to perform some movements that you won't understand. When led of the Spirit this is a faith walk of obedience. All interpretation belongs to the Lord.
As you exercise this type of prophetic movement and seek the Lord for His interpretation, you will increase your vocabulary of symbolism. We can develop a skill in this area like Daniel as he became skillful in the interpretation of symbols in dreams.
Dan.1: 7 "…as for these children, God gave him knowledge and skill in all learning and wisdom: and Daniel had understanding in all visions and dreams." Skill: distinction, discernment

understanding, a developed or acquired ability. *Webster's Dictionary.*
We do understand that all knowledge of dream interpretation comes from the Lord.
 The Lord is no respecter of persons, as we humble ourselves, read His word and ask to be vessels used for His purposes, He will give us understanding and wisdom.

Scripture reveals that every symbolic action directed by the Lord has a corresponding heavenly reaction.

The Israelites were well aware of this and put the worshippers before their army, to create the atmosphere, which would invite the presence of the Lord.
 2nd.Chron.20: 21 Jehosaphat consulted with the people, he appointed singers unto the Lord that should praise the beauty of holiness, as they went out before the army, and to say Praise the Lord for His mercy endureth forever. When they began to sing and praise the Lord, the Lord set ambushes against the children of Ammon, Moab and Mt.Seir, which were come against Judah; and they were smitten.

They claimed the mercy of God in a spirit of repentance for their own sins so they wouldn't be wiped out along with their enemies.
Ps 103:20 "Bless the Lord, ye his angels that excel in strength, that do his commandments, hearkening unto the voice of his word."

8

Chapter 3
Willing Vessels

Rom 12:1 "I beseech you therefore, brethren, by the mercies of God, that ye present your bodies a living sacrifice, holy, acceptable unto God, which is your reasonable service."
We are to present our bodies as living sacrifices. The word "service" is the Greek word latriah meaning "ministration of God, worship, (divine service) render homage." *Strongs concordance*

Worship and praise was and is meant to be pro-active, a demonstration of thanksgiving and praise in faith.

The Lord is the same yesterday, today, and forever. He won't be changing the way He desires us to worship him. This is not man's idea, but God's instruction.
In Israel today at celebrations, there is a dancing demonstration of praise and worship much like the Old and New Testament worshippers.
This emotional demonstration of praise and worship might be a new concept to some of us, but has been a normal act of worship to the Jewish people for over two thousand years!

1 Peter 2:9 "But ye are a chosen generation, a royal priesthood, an holy nation, a peculiar people; that ye should show forth the praises of him who hath called you out of darkness into his marvelous light."
At times, we can look pretty peculiar as we "show forth" the praises of God. Showing forth is defined as: "The point whence motion or action proceeds from; demonstrate, display, exhibit, to manifest a performance as proof of the actuality or existence of something." *Webster's Dictionary.*
Manifested (Praise): evidence to the senses and to the sight; not obscure. *Webster's Dictionary.*
My definition would be: A public demonstration of power and purpose. An exercise of faith, spirit, soul, and body!

9

Heavenly Impact

In the case of public manifested praise, worship, or intercession, some symbolic acts won't make sense to those around you. Exercise wisdom, be sensitive, and use common sense.

Symbolic acts that are universal.

Water Baptism: symbolizing the burying of our old carnal nature, rising up to walk in newness of life in Jesus. *Mark 1:4.*

Anointing with oil: throughout the word this represented a symbol of the seal of approval from the Lord upon a person who was being consecrated to an office. *Ex 28:41.* Also used to symbolize the Holy Spirit.

Communion: the bread symbolizing the body of Christ and the wine or juice symbolizing His blood shed for our redemption from sin. *Matt 26:26.*

These are just to name a few that most Christians enact today on a regular basis, and will continue to do so until Jesus returns.

In the Old Testament, the majority of the symbolic acts we read about usually were performed as a result of a desperate situation. God's people needed deliverance from their enemies. The Lord set the stage by orchestrating an impossible situation so that His people knew their deliverance could only come from Him. As they repented and were restored spiritually to Him, the Lord would move miraculously on their behalf.
As the Lord instructed his earthly delegate to perform a symbolic action, with a symbolic tool, there was an immediate activation of the heavenly host, accompanied by a direct repercussion felt or seen upon the earth.

Anything could happen and it did!

 In some cases, the Spirit of the Lord came upon an ambassador person enabling him to do great exploits.

Judges 6:34 "But the Spirit of the Lord came upon Gideon, and he blew a trumpet; and Abiezer (the father of help) was gathered after him." (Parentheses mine, Abiezer is #44 in the Hebrew language from Strong's Concordance: The Father of help.) In the account of the victory of Gideon's men over their enemies, symbolic spiritual weapons were used as God's tools of judgment.

Throughout scripture God identifies Himself through the voice of the shofar. (Shofar chapter.) This was a proof to Gideon that the Lord was with him. The Lord always responds in some manner to the blowing of the shofar.
Our commander and chief, the Lord Sabboath, the Lord of the Hosts, rides instantly to our defense on the wings of the clouds. His army is with him.

Judges 7:9 "And it came to pass the same night, that the Lord said unto him, Arise, get thee down unto the host; for I have delivered it into thine hand."

Judges 7:20-21 "And the three companies blew the trumpets, and brake the pitchers, and held the lamps in their left hands, and the trumpets in their right hands to blow withal: and they cried, The sword of the Lord, and of Gideon. And they stood every man in his place round about the camp: and all the host ran, and cried, and fled."

Neh 4:20 "In what place therefore ye hear the sound of the trumpet, resort ye thither unto us: our God shall fight for us."

Heavenly Impact

In this story, the enemy went into a panic due to the presence of the Lord coming into their camp.
Gideon's army shouted "The sword of the Lord" to give a voice to the <u>prophetic</u> <u>word</u> of God that was spoken to Gideon earlier that night. (The word of God is described as a sword Ps. 149:6.)

 As the men blew the shofars, the Lord also blew a shofar announcing His presence.
"And the Lord shall be seen over them, and his arrow shall go forth as lightning: and the Lord God shall blow the trumpet, and shall go with the whirlwinds of the south." Zech 9:14.
The men held up torches symbolizing the fire of the zeal of God. As they declared the word of the Lord, and blew the shofars, the heavenly host was sent into the enemy camp!
 Ps 103:20 "Bless the Lord, ye his angels that excel in strength, that do his commandments, hearkening unto the voice of his word."

One of the reasons that Gideon included himself in the declaration, "The sword of the Lord and of Gideon" was to make it clear that when you blend the word of God with man's obedience, you get victory.

The Lord calls us to co-labor with Him in the battles that we face. Maybe we are to depend on Him in a way we never have before, not to take on the battle ourselves, but to announce the Lord's presence onto the scene, worshipping as He defeats our spiritual enemies before us!

Chapter 4
The Tabret
תבר

"Dancing in the River flowing from the throne"

Heavenly Impact

The ancient instrument called the tabret played an important role in worship and praise of the Lord God of Israel. It was commonly used in ancient days, but has largely disappeared from the scene over the centuries in most parts of the earth. Jer. 31:4 speaks prophetically of the restoration of the tabret to the Lord's worshipping bride before the return of the Messiah (Jesus).

"Again I will build thee, and thou shalt be built, O virgin of Israel: thou shalt be again adorned with thy tabrets, and shalt go forth in the dances of them that make merry." KJV.

According to scripture the tabret and the pipe were the first instruments created by God to be used to praise and glorify Him. (Ezek. 28:13-explained later in the chapter). The revelation of the impact made in the heavenlies as we worship and praise with the tabret on the earth will be clearly shown in scripture throughout this chapter.

My first contact with the symbolic prophetic instrument called the tabret was in 1996 during a Sunday evening worship service at our church. I noticed that someone had placed a wooden embroidery hoop decorated with colorful streamers of mylar, sometimes called tinsel on the alter steps.

While I was worshipping before the Lord in the dance I picked up the beautiful hoop and began to twirl around with it. Suddenly the Holy Spirit spoke to my heart and said; "I am going to use these to set my people free in worship, and as a vehicle of cross pollination for revival throughout the lands."

I was shocked! I thought, what is this instrument? It must be important to the Lord. Later I asked the lady who had set the hoop on the alter what it was. She said that it was called a Glory hoop. She had just returned from Israel and had used it there and brought it back with her.

14

The Tabret

It was a dance adornment, but she didn't know if it had any specific scriptural significance. Later that evening I shared with my husband what the Lord had spoken to me.

We prayed for the Lord to reveal to us if we were to play a part in this prophetic word concerning this instrument, and where it was spoken of in His word. A few of us women began to make these hoops and wave them in our church with our pastors blessing.

We stretched fabric across the center of the hoop and wrote scripture or put symbolic appliqués on them to convey a biblical message. We would wave them as a wave offering unto the Lord. The positive result from the use of these hoops was a higher level of active participation on the part of the congregation during praise and worship.

As more people would join in waving the hoops during praise, some who had been very reserved in worship began to become less inhibited, more active and expressive as they picked up these hoops and waved them.

People who visited our church wanted to know more about the hoops and wanted to have them to take back to their churches. We saw the effect that these simple, but powerful, point of contact hoops had on a person as they used them in praise and worship. Several months later I was asked to share with a church women's group on the subject of worship. I was looking up the word worship in a little King James computer that I carry.

1st.Sam.18: 6 came up. (This was a miracle in itself because this scripture doesn't contain the word worship).

1st. Sam.18:6 "And it came to pass as they came, when David was returned from the slaughter of the Philistine, that the women came out of all the cities of Israel, singing and dancing, to meet King Saul, with tabrets, with joy, and with instruments of music. And the women answered one another as they played and said, Saul hath slain his thousands, and David his ten thousands "

Heavenly Impact

The definition of tabret revealed a description that matched these symbolic instruments we were using in praise.
Tabret-A small tabor.
Tabor-A small drum with one head, taboret-A small tabor, small seat without arms or back, <u>also</u> <u>a</u> <u>small</u> <u>light</u> <u>frame</u> <u>for</u> <u>holding</u> <u>material</u> <u>while</u> <u>being</u> <u>upholstered;</u> see tabour.
Tabour-A drum. <u>A</u> <u>circular</u> <u>frame</u> <u>consisting</u> <u>of</u> <u>two</u> <u>hoops</u> <u>one</u> <u>fitting</u> <u>within</u> <u>the</u> <u>other</u> <u>in</u> <u>which</u> <u>cloth</u> <u>is</u> <u>stretched</u> <u>for</u> <u>embroidery.</u>
Crystal Reference Online Dictionary.

 The ancient original form of the tabret was a small, rustic one-sided drum. It had a leather strap attached. It was slung from the shoulder of the players left arm and was beaten either by a stick held in the right hand, or by the right hand itself. At the same time the taborer played a pipe held to his mouth by
his other hand. The Israelites associated its use with processions, and with joy, feasting and mirth. (P.117. *Groves Dictionaries of Music Inc. New York, N.Y. Macmillan Press Limited 1984.*)

After much prayer and fasting concerning the word of the Lord to us about these hoops, and the reference in these definitions which describe the hoops we are using, we fully believe them to be
 a symbolic forerunner of the ancient instrument called a tabret (tabor) in the scripture. I believe the Hebrew women decorated them much like we do. They may have had different colored streamers of various materials hanging down from them.

I believe the women, no matter what generation they would be born into, would want to put some color and decoration to their instrument. The meanings of the colors of the streamers are as important today as they were then. They have a symbolic meaning to the person using the tabret.
The colors have special meaning to the Lord also. He was specific about the colors to use in the tabernacle, which spoke a voiceless language to those who had an understanding of symbolism.

16

The Tabret

After this revelation the Lord put a mandate on my heart to co-labor with him in the adorning and equipping of His bride. To adorn by providing these symbolic items, to equip by teaching the biblical roots of the item and the heavenly impact that is made when we use them.

Below are the nine scriptures in the modern King James Version of 1611 that contain the word tabret. They reveal its different functions and importance as it is used.

The Tabret is used with other instruments to prepare the atmosphere for the Spirit of Prophecy, to overtake the setting.

1 Sam. 10:5-6: "After that thou shalt come to the hill of God, where is the garrison of the Philistines; and it shall come to pass, when thou art come thither to the city, that thou shalt meet a company of prophets coming down from the high place with a psaltry, and a tabret, and a pipe, and a harp before them; and they shall prophesy. Then the spirit of the Lord will possess you and you will be in a prophetic frenzy along with them, and be turned into a different person. NRSV.

After Samuel anointed Saul to be king over Israel, he directed Saul to go to a specific geographical location, where he knew the prophets would be. These prophets were coming down from the high place of worship, with praisers leading the way, spiritually preparing the atmosphere for the presence of the Lord. Corporate unity in worship is powerful. The same holds true today. If you place yourself in this anointed atmosphere of worship, and are willing you may be turned into a new man as Saul was.

17

Heavenly Impact

1 Sam.18:6 "And it came to pass as they came, when David was returned from the slaughter of the Philistine, that the women came out of all the cities of Israel, singing and dancing, to meet King Saul, with tabrets, with joy, and with instruments of music.
And the women answered one another as they played and said Saul hath slain his thousands, and David his tens of thousands."

As the women used these prophetic instruments, the spirit of prophecy came upon them, and they began to prophesy. They were prophetically inspired to ascribe victory to David for thousands yet to come, as though they already were.
They were calling the prophetic future tense into the present tense, as the Holy Spirit came upon them. Saul understood and believed that what they prophesied came from God, so it would come to pass.
 As the Restoration of the Tabernacle of David with Davidic style of worship increases throughout the land, the tabret or tabor as a drum will begin to appear and we will begin to corporately use them as a natural part of our worship ordained of God.

It is wonderful to understand that as we wave the symbolic tabrets in worship prophetically, they are sending forth a signal or vibration like a radio wave, into the atmosphere, calling forth prophetically the restoration of their ancient counterpart, the drum or tabor.
This waving of a symbolic item wasn't unusual to the Hebrew children. In the New Testament, Mark 14:65 describes believers waving palm branches and throwing their outer garments down on the road before Jesus the King as he rode in to town.
Rev.7:9 describes the saints in the throne room waving palm branches, and casting crowns down that are in their hands as a symbol of worship and adoration.

The Tabret

Tabrets used during times of celebration

Gen.31:27 "Wherefore didst thou flee away secretly, and steal away from me, and didst not tell me, that I might have sent thee away with mirth (joy, merriment), and with songs, with tabret and with harp?"
Isa. 24:8 "The mirth of the tabrets ceaseth, the noise of them that rejoice endeth, the joy of the harp ceaseth."

We must not forget the reason for the celebration.

Isa.5:12 "And the harp, and the viol, the tabret, and pipe, and wine, are in their feasts: but they regard not the work of the Lord, neither consider the operation of His hands."

Any good thing taken to the excess can become an abuse. This is what the enemy wants and we must guard against putting too much emphasis upon anything but the Lord.

Tabret recognized in ancient days as an object of beauty.

Job 17:6 "He hath made me also a byword of the people and aforetime I was as a tabret." Def. of byword: an object of scorn. Def. of aforetime: A time in the past. *Webster's Dictionary.*
Here Job is saying that in the past, his life had been a praise and an object of beauty, before the Lord and the people, likened to a tabret. At this time in Job's life he is an object of scorn in front of the people, but before, when he was being blessed and favored by God he was as a tabret. This, once again, speaks of the tabret as an object of beauty, of which Job and his friends are obviously familiar.

Heavenly Impact

Strongs concordance gives another number for the word tabret in this scripture ref. #8611 topheth; a smiting from #8606 -to drum. My opinion is that the scripture could be translated that aforetime the Lord used me as a tabret; I was a vessel of His glory used to proclaim His word. With every beat of my heart the rhythm of God's life flowed out through me for others to clearly see the Lord's blessings and favor. As the beat of my heart praised the Lord it was as a smiting to my enemies. Now I am as an object of scorn before the people.

When God created the first worship leader of heavens choirs He placed the tabret within his framework.

Ezek 28:13 Thou hast been in Eden the garden of God; every precious stone was thy covering, the sardius, topaz, and the diamond, the beryl, the onyx, and the jasper, the sapphire, the emerald, and the carbuncle, and gold: The workmanship of thy tabrets and of thy pipes was prepared in thee in the day that thou wast created.

According to many biblical resources, this scripture is speaking of lucifer. "Every precious stone was your covering." (Unlike man who was created naked). The main thing to note is regardless of whether the being described in this scripture is human or angelic, he was created by the Lord with a tabret within him to be able to express worship and praise the way the Lord wanted it expressed. This expression of worship is formed through vibration creating sound waves. The high order and specific placement of lucifer prior to his fall afforded unique opportunity to bring glory to God. Musical reference (pipes) in this chapter and verse suggests his role included leading heaven's choirs in the worship of the Most High God.
His fall was occasioned by his seeking to have this glory for himself. *Commentary from the Spirit Filled Life Bible.*

The Tabret

These tabrets play an important role in worship. The Lord ordained and approves of their use. He created them to be used for this purpose. The Lord has given this responsibility and honor of worship, praise and intercession of the Most High God to us.

<u>Tabrets are an offensive weapon in the spiritual kingdom! The Lord Himself lays the tabret on the back of the enemy as we praise!</u>

We see in the scripture that these instruments serve a dual spiritual purpose: One is to worship and praise the Lord. The other is to make a declaration of atmospheric change pertaining to the symbolism on the face of them. This symbolic written description or picture can turn them into an offensive weapon in the spiritual realm.

For example, The sequined flames of fire that are on the face of the tabret you are waving is a declaration or invitation for the Holy Spirit to come into your midst and refine your tabernacle (spirit, soul, and body) with a refining fire, to bring along the Spirit of revival fire. This same fire will burn up the enemy if he is anywhere around! The intercession tabret has a brass sword, and arrow and a battle-axe of the Lord on it.

Isa.31:8 Then shall the Assyrian fall with the sword, not of a mighty man; and the sword, not of a mean man, shall devour him: but he shall flee from the sword, and his young men shall be discomfited.

Isa 30:32 "And in every place where the grounded staff (staff of punishment, the word of God) shall pass, <u>which the Lord shall lay upon him</u>, it shall be <u>with tabrets</u> and harps; and in battles of shaking (brandishing) will He fight with it."
Def. of brandish: To wave or flourish triumphantly, or flourish as with a weapon. *Webster's Dictionary.*

21

Heavenly Impact

As we flourish and wave the tabret unto the Lord in worship and praise, glorifying him with our mouths and our hands, the Lord is using it in the heavenly realm on the back of our enemy! Even though we are focused on worship, we are patterning here on the earth what our father is doing in the heavens against our enemy. He and his host are executing the judgment written against our enemies as we sing and speak the word in praise and worship.

With the illumination of the scripture we become armed with a method to measure the impact we are making in the heavenlies, as a result of our action on the earth.

Our focus is to praise and worship the Lord. As we do this we are creating a resting place for the Lord on one hand, and causing our enemies to panic and flee on the other. What a joy!

Restoration of the Tabrets to the Bride prophesied.

My question to the Lord as I was researching was "Where have they been?" We have had the tambourine all along why not the tabret? The answer was found in the last scripture I looked up. *Jer.31:4 "Again I will build thee, and thou shalt be built, O virgin of Israel, thou shalt again be adorned with thy tabrets, and shall go forth in the dances of them that make merry."*
Shalt again means to bring back something.

This is an end-time prophecy now being fulfilled as we wave our symbolic tabrets, much as our brothers and sisters of ancient days waved the palm branches and sheaves of grain as wave offerings before the Lord. We are proclaiming:
Rev.22: 17 "The Spirit and the Bride say come Lord Jesus!"

The Tabret

The Lord is restoring the tabret to His dancing bride before He returns. It is ancient and modern custom to bring a gift if you are able to have an audience with the king. He is giving us these adornments as gifts that we in turn are using to prepare the way for Him. We have been given the honor of leading the choirs of heaven and earth in worship and praise to the Most High God!

This is a slap in the face to the enemy as we wave these tabrets in praise. He knows they are symbolic forerunners of the ancient tabret or drum; he is reminded of what he once had and was stripped of, and his impending future.

Tabret, Timbrel, Tambourine?

We sought the Lord in prayer for an explanation of why the word tabret read timbrel or tambourine in most translations. The answer was found in an old Bible. It states the following: There are more than 500 words that today are considered to be archaic and obsolete to the modern day reader. These words have been changed to help the modern day average reader to more readily understand their meaning. In this list of 500 words is the word tabret. It says the word tabret has been changed to read timbrel or tambourine in most translations. *The Holy Bible illustrated containing the Old and New testaments translated out of the original tongues and with the former translations diligently compared and revised. King James Version 1611.*

There are nine specific scriptures according to the original texts which use the word tabret instead of timbrel or tambourine. The word still correctly reads tabret in *King James versions,* including the *Hebrew/Greek study Bible.*
The root word for timbrel is toph or tuppim, different than the root word of the tabret which is tabor.

Heavenly Impact

There are ten scriptures concerning the timbrel or tambourine. We see the mention of the tabret and pipe often used together in scripture, unlike the timbrel which is played alone.

In many different locations throughout the earth the tabrets (tabors) are now being restored and used as they were in ancient days. The actual tabor or tabret is not an instrument that everyone could pick up and play musically, as a drum, without some training. Anyone can wave these forerunner symbolic point of contact tabrets.

Children, senior citizens, those in wheelchairs even those lying upon their beds. It is possible for anyone to move into a new dimension of expressive boldness resembling the style of worship the Hebrew children exercised. Because they are basically soundless you can't get off beat with them.

Below are several testimonies about these symbolic tabrets.

A pastor's wife from Oregon wrote a letter to share a testimony concerning the heavenly impact of the use of symbolic instruments in their church.

The church had invited a man, who had been delivered out of the occult, and become a Christian, to teach on strategies of intercession. After the main speaking part of the program, the congregation was praying for their state leaders and the leaders of the state next to them. There is a river that flows in the natural between these two states. The Holy Spirit led them to perform a symbolic enactment. To form a bridge in the physical realm symbolizing a bridge in the spiritual realm, so these states would prophetically become united in the spirit to effect some changes in the physical. The congregation members symbolically enacted this by using two chairs which they laid down on the floor across from each other.

The front of the seats were on the floor and the tops of the backs meeting together in the air which formed a type of symbolic bridge to proclaim a bridge of connection in the physical/spiritual realm.

The Tabret

Then they laid a piece of blue fabric under the chairs symbolizing the river. They laid flags over the chairs and waved tabrets and flags over it all, dancing around and praising the Lord while quoting particular prophetic scriptures concerning the unity of the two states and the anointing for the completion of God's purposes that would flow from this prophetic act.

The guest speaker shared afterward how he had a new age occult magazine that he used as example for testimony when this type of symbolic intercession occurred in a church where he was speaking. He got the magazine out and read a letter written to the editor. It was written from a person requesting advice concerning the confusion he was experiencing in the spiritual realm due to Christians using symbolic items in their worship. Their style of praise was creating a disruption in his spiritual communications and brought much confusion to the airwaves! How awesome is that!
A good example of this would be when you are driving; listening to a radio station, when suddenly another station comes on and you can't hear the one you were listening to. The second one overpowers the first one's signal. That's how we are changing the atmosphere as we utilize these tools of symbolism with praise.
 We see examples of this confusion coming into the enemy camp during the use of symbolic instruments in the account of Gideon and his men blowing on shofars and holding up lights. The enemy became confused and turned on each other with their weapons, and slaughtered themselves. *Judges 7:20.*

Another testimony.
While at a Prophetic conference several of us women were standing at the display table which was in the hallway outside the conference room. The symbolic tabrets were lying along the front of the table. As a group of ladies were walking by, the lady closest to the table suddenly brushed her hand against one of the tabrets which is called Celebration Jubilee: freedom from bondage.

(We give the tabrets symbolic names.) She suddenly jumped back and yelled at the same time bumping into the ladies who were walking with her. She looked at me, pointed to a tabret and said, "What is that thing?" I said, "It is a symbolic worship item used during praise and worship of the Lord." With a shocked look she said, "It just bit me on the hand!"
We hadn't had that happen before. I told her that if that thing had bitten her then I would say the Lord had arrested her that day for a reason. I told her that it was used as a point of contact and shared a few scriptures with her about the tabret. She was very interested. I asked her if she would like me to pray for her. She said yes. We stepped around behind the wall into a stairwell and I asked her how she would like me to pray for her. She said "Just pray however you think." I told her that I would just wait a moment to ask the Holy Spirit how to pray for her. I began to pray in unknown tongues silently for her. As I did this she began to weep. The Holy Spirit spoke to my heart and said this lady is involved in witchcraft.

I asked her if she knew who Jesus was. She said yes that she had been raised in the church. She went on to say that when she was about 13 -14 years old (30) years ago, she would hear words in her mind about the people who were receiving prayer. As a young Christian she thought this was wonderful and that she should speak these things to the people.
She would tell the people what she knew about them, good and bad. The people didn't like this, they became afraid of her. She was expelled from the church and was labeled a witch and she said she hadn't been back.

  I explained to her that she had been given a prophetic gifting from the Lord which the church at that time obviously didn't recognize or know what to do with. I told her that Jesus was grieved over this lack of knowledge concerning her prophetic gifting. He loved her and obviously wanted her in His kingdom. When I asked her if she wanted to use her prophetic gifting for Jesus. Her reply surprised me. She said; "I can't, I have sold my soul to satan." I told her that when Jesus died on the cross he paid for her sins, if she repented of her sins asking forgiveness then she would be bought back by Jesus. She began to cry and asked if this was true? "Can I come back to Jesus after all I have done?" I prayed with her; she repented and she was restored to the Lord.

Later she explained that she worked for the sheriff's dept. The terminology that I had innocently used about the Lord arresting her had pierced her heart. She knew God was talking to her. She explained that this would make a big change in her life because she was using her prophetic gift to make extra money telling fortunes at the jail. We introduced her to the pastor in charge of the prophetic giftings conference. She came to every night meeting that week. When I heard from her last she was still in that church and walking with the Lord. She bought a Celebration Jubilee Tabret to wave!

Performing Symbolic Enactments with these Instruments.

Symbolic enactments of the divine nature need to be handled carefully and fearfully. For every action there is a reaction or repercussion in the physical and spiritual realm. The scriptures give testimony that when a person is inspired by the Holy Spirit to perform a divinely directed enactment, there is an anointing that can be directed as an arrow, towards a target.

The Arrow of the Lord.

You as the bow, performing the physical movement, the arrow hits its target in the spiritual realm causing the repercussion to be felt and seen in the physical (earthly) realm.

This is a testimony concerning the symbolic enactment of shooting an arrow in the physical sense for spiritual reasons or effects, to reveal the unseen heavenly reality which parallels the visible.   In the past years I have seen at conferences and other intercession meetings people enacting the shooting of spiritual arrows. Out of genuine concern I share these testimonies of both positive and negative effects of shooting spiritual arrows.

Positive Effect:
One Sunday evening we had a visitor at our church that went forward to receive prayer. I had never seen the man before this night. The pastor anointed him with oil and the intercessors gathered around him to pray. I was over in the front corner of the church dancing with an intercession tabret. This tabret has a symbolic arrow of the Lord on it. The Holy Spirit quickened me to go over and dance quietly around the circle of intercessors surrounding the visitor.

As I was dancing around the outer perimeter of the circle there was an open space directly behind the visitor. The Holy Spirit spoke to my heart and said, "Slide into that space." As I was slowly waving the tabret and praying in the spirit, as the rest of the group was, the Holy Spirit said "Shoot him with an arrow." I thought I was hearing things at first because I hadn't ever done anything like this. I inquired of the Holy Spirit "What do you want me to put on this arrow?" He said, "encouragement and victory." I looked around to see that everyone had their eyes closed, they did.

The Tabret

I drew up my left hand and pulled back my right hand about waist high and said quietly. "The arrow of the Lord sent forth unto you, encouragement and victory is yours, receive it into your spirit", then I released the spiritual arrow.

   There was an immediate reaction not only from the man, whose feet flew out from under him, down he went and began bouncing on the floor, the pastor and each intercessor all grabbed their stomachs and bent over with a shout like they had each been struck by an arrow, all at the same time!
I also had an immediate reaction. I turned and went <u>quickly</u> back over to my corner praying in the spirit, flourishing those tabrets up and down and all around, wondering about what had just happened. The man continued bouncing up and down on the floor on his back while the group moved on to another man. The same thing happened again, The Holy Spirit instructed me to dance around the group then slide into an open space behind the man and to shoot an arrow of healing, which I did and there was a repeat of what happened to the first man. Both men were bouncing up and down for several minutes after being shot.

After the prayer service I reported to the pastor what had happened. He told me that when he had been standing in front of the visitor praying for him, he felt like he had been hit in the stomach with an arrow.

Six weeks later the visitor and his wife showed up once again on a Sunday night. I went to them to introduce myself and ask the man if he had gotten an answer to his prayer that he had been seeking the last time they visited. He replied that yes, a real miracle had occurred. He shared with me that he was a pastor from another town. His mission was to specific tribes of Native American Indians in a western state. His goal was to help them put together a big peace meeting involving several tribes that had not been able to get along for many generations. It was to be a healing time of reconciliation.

Heavenly Impact

He had been working on this project about a year. That day he had received a call that there had been a problem and the whole project had been canceled. He said that he had come to church that night discouraged and quite ready to give it up. After receiving prayer he felt like a great burden had been lifted.

The next day he had received a phone call that all had been settled and the meeting would go on as planned. The meeting did in fact happen with major breakthroughs and victories. He had come back to praise the Lord with us for the victory.
I shared with him what the Holy Spirit had told me to do. He looked at his wife and said "Didn't I tell you it felt like I had been shot with an arrow of hope?" She nodded her head yes. I thought it interesting that the Lord had me use an arrow when his ministry was to the Indians.

The other man who was shot with the arrow of healing has a disease which the doctors told him would put him in a wheelchair by now, which hasn't happened. We still pray for a complete healing for him and expect to see it come to pass.

As intercessors we began to seek direction through the scriptures about shooting the Lord's arrows and found examples of where the Lord had used a human ambassador to shoot arrows for His purposes.
2 kings 13: 15-19 And Elisha said unto him, Take the bow and arrows. and he took unto him bow and arrows and he said to the King of Israel, put thy hand upon the bow, and he put his hand upon it; and Elisha put his hands upon the king's hands. And he said open the window eastward. and he opened it. Then he said, "Shoot!" So he did.
Then Elisha proclaimed, "This is the Lord's arrow, full of victory over Aram, for you will completely conquer the Arameans at Aphek". New Living Translation.

The Tabret

As we read on further we see in verse 18 how important it is to be sensitive and obedient to the instruction of the Holy Spirit when performing a symbolic enactment. We follow instructions exactly. No more or no less.
Vs.18 and he said, take the arrows. And he took them. And he said unto the king of Israel, Smite upon the ground, and he smote thrice, and stayed. And the man of God was wroth with him, and said, Thou shouldest have smitten five or six times; then hast thou smitten Syria till thou hadst consumed it; whereas now thou shalt smite Syria but thrice.

As we speak forth the word of the Lord (scripture) symbolically placing it in arrow form to be shot we become the polished shaft in His quiver.
Is.49:2 And He hath made my mouth like a sharp sword; in the shadow of his hand hath he hid me, and made me a polished shaft; in his quiver hath he hid me.

If a Christian symbolically enacts shooting an arrow at another Christian, it could be spiritually deadly, at the least painful for both. Symbolic arrows should never be shot carelessly without a specific God ordained target or a word from the Holy Spirit of what to say prophetically. When shot at another Christian brother or sister they should always be shot through the leading of the Holy Spirit and with the purpose of bringing edification. In the spirit, I have seen many people including Christians, walking around with arrows sticking out of them all over.

If you are in pain with no visible explanation, you may want to seek the Lord, asking if this could be the root of the pain. You could have been shot by an arrow from the tongue.
Ps. 64:3-4 Who whet their tongue like a sword, and bend their bows to shoot their arrows, even bitter words: That they may shoot in secret at the perfect: suddenly do they shoot at him, and fear not.

Heavenly Impact

After sharing this story with a friend who was having severe back and shoulder pain that had come on her suddenly six months earlier we prayed symbolically removing arrows from the areas of the pain, then symbolically poured oil of healing into those sites quoting healing scriptures over her. She said the pain left immediately. (I am not saying that anyone in pain has been shot or has shot an arrow at someone, but why take the chance?) There is an arrow of God's divine judgment. Only you can discern if you may have moved into a position where the Lord has to judge you. This would give the enemy a legal right to hurt you in this way. Gossip or judging others would be examples.

Ps.64:5-7 they *encourage themselves in an evil matter: they commune of laying snares privily; they say, Who shall see them? search out iniquities; they accomplish a diligent search: both the inward thought of every one of them, and the heart, is deep. But God shall shoot at them with an arrow; suddenly shall they be wounded.*
There may be someone reading this who is thinking,
" I am guilty of this type of offense (gossip, slander)." If you are guilty, immediately seek the Lord in repentance confessing this sin before the Lord, asking the Lord to forgive you.
The word says that we will give an account for every word we have spoken. *Matt.12:36.* By our words we will be justified or condemned.
Prayer: "Lord I come before you with a repentant heart. I have sinned against you and against my brother with my tongue. Forgive me and cleanse me with the blood of Jesus, thus moving me from a cursed state into a state of blessing. In your grace and mercy please allow me to remove those arrows of bitter/slanderous words from my brother." Spiritually enact pulling the arrow out of the person.

The Tabret

Fill the wounded site by blessing the brother or sister. An example would be: "Father send your healing touch to my brother/sister right now. Cleanse their wounds with your blood, set them free in Jesus' name. Amen." If possible (not always necessary), ask the person to forgive you of words that you have spoken (unless the Lord tells you to go into detail, don't.)

Scriptures concerning the arrow of the Lord to be used during times of intercession, by intercessors.

The Lord's ordained arrow is His word quoted in the mouth of an intercessor which when spoken becomes a winged word arrow against the enemy.

Ps. 7:11 God judgeth the righteous and God is angry with the wicked every day. If he turn not he will whet his sword; He hath bent his bow and made it ready. He hath also prepared for him the instruments of death; He ordaineth his arrows against the persecutors.

Hab.3:11 The lofty sun and moon began to fade, obscured by brilliance from your arrows and the flashing of your glittering spear. NLT.
Zach.9:14 Then the Lord will be seen over them, and His arrow will go forth like lightning. The Lord God will blow the trumpet, and go with whirlwinds from the south. King James Version

The enemy shoots arrows

It is important to put on our spiritual armor everyday, to keep ourselves under the protection of the Lord by living a righteous life unto the Lord.

Ps.37:12-15 The wicked plots against the just, and gnashes at him. The Lord laughs at him for he sees that his day is coming. The wicked have bent their bow to cast down the poor and needy, to slay those who are of upright conduct. Their sword shall enter their own heart, and their bows shall be broken.
Ps.11:2 For look! The wicked bend their bow; they make ready their arrow on the string that they may shoot secretly at the upright in heart.

Symbolic movements

Below are a few examples of symbolic movements that are performed with the tabrets. The Lord will give you more as you use them. Many people are making these movements, but have told us they didn't understand what they were doing. When you have understanding of the prophetic movements you are making you will surely move with a definite purpose! Most of these movements we make with a tabret in each hand, but of course can be done with one tabret.

"Waves of Glory."

You hold a tabret in each hand and make circles that flow in an outward motion away from your body. Your hands would move from a close together position to far apart. You can do this low then high in a continuous motion.

"Cutting off from the enemy."

A tabret in each hand usually, arms waving up and down stiffly at your side. As you walk forward your right foot steps out the left arm goes up then down as the left foot steps forward, and right hand goes up higher that your head.

The Tabret

It looks like the exaggerated movement you used to see of military ranks as they walked and swung their arms.
You can walk from a center point north, south, east and west making this cutting off movement to symbolize a setting free of the captives. To complete the movement you can walk in a circle around all of this symbolizing the Lords omnipotence. You would swing your arms up and down in a slicing cutting off motion. You can also swing them in a horizontal movement also.

"Revolution."

You hold your hands up in the air while turning in circles. You are revolutionizing the atmosphere, and your life. God is turning situations around for victory.

"Wave offering."

This was done with a sheave of grain held in the hands and waved before the Lord. Place your two hands close together, waving your hands back and forth above or in front of you with the tabret. Turn the hoop up on its side so it is horizontal with a hand on either side, lifting it up above our heads unto the Lord, moving the tabret from side to side rocking on our feet back and forth as we do this.
You can turn in circles with it held in this way above your head symbolizing that you are turning your thoughts and meditations upon Him as you offer up your praise unto Him. Bowing down smoothly, lay the tabret out on the floor symbolizing the humbling of ourselves before the Lord.
Laying all earthly burdens before Him, and give praise for His divine purpose to be accomplished through you.
You can lift the tabret above your head while in this bowing posture also. Hands up are a universal movement for surrender.

Heavenly Impact

"Butterfly Flourish."

When you wave the tabret in a circle eight movement it symbolizes that something is never-ending. An example would be the love of Christ and His mighty hand upon your life is never ending. His mercy endureth forever. You can perform this continuous movement in front of you or at the sides, as you spin around in a circle or above your head.

You can do this with a tabret in each hand; wave with one tabret following the other in the motion or you can spread your hands apart and cross over each other moving back and forth.

"Ascending in worship movement."

Hands in front of you making a loop around each other starting low, advancing upwards symbolizing our song unto the Lord. When we reverse this movement we are symbolizing receiving from the Lord. This is a beautiful movement to symbolize water flowing also. You can move in a circle while doing this, hands can begin at any level with this movement, the lower you start it the more effective it is. When you do this while turning in circles it is quite beautiful and expressive to use a stair step effect as you are turning, up, then down, continuous movement with a tabret in each hand.

"The Lord is our rock movement"

Hold your left hand in a horizontal extended position in front of you, if a tabret is in that hand lay it on its side. (vertically). Make a wide exaggerated forward circle on your right side with your right hand. As you bring your right hand around make a fist and bring it down on the face of the tabret, or your open palm that is extended out in front of you, then turn both hands palms down and sweep in opposite directions away, then begin another movement.

The Tabret

"Threshing the harvest"

As you grasp the tabret, make a motion as if you are threshing grain. A swooshing movement from up by your shoulder across and down in front of your body. You can do this with both hands. You are prophetically threshing a harvest of souls into the kingdom.

"The sweep"

Sweep the tabret from side to side to sweep the atmosphere. The intercessors sometimes sweep through the sanctuary before church doing this sweeping movement to cleanse the atmosphere.

The sweep was one of those movements you do without thinking much about it. While watching a morning show several years back there was a women from England who is the author of a book that exposes the witchcraft that is being taught to children in the Harry Potter series. She shared that when the cover of one of the books came out the witches put up a big fuss and threatened to sue because the cover showed Harry riding a broom.

They said it was an incorrect picture because the bristles were at the back and should be at the front, to sweep the atmosphere before them. That gives new meaning to this movement.

These are just a few movements. As you use the tabrets the Lord will give you more. Most of the movements with all of the instruments are interchangeable. This means you can use the tool of choice in your hand to do any of the movements.

In 1997 my husband and I formed a company called Glorious Creations. We are dedicated to co-labor with the Lord to fulfill the prophetic word given to me. Almost immediately a team developed.

Heavenly Impact

We work together creating, praying blessings over and sending tabrets with their scriptural validation papers to the very ends of the earth, with testimonies echoing back of revival being activated in the hearts of those using them. We are so grateful to the Lord for such an opportunity to be used in this way as He adorns His bride for His return.

I pray that this chapter will be a great blessing to those who have also been called to this adorning of the bride, and may have been actively involved in their ministry, and to those who have felt the call, but haven't activated themselves in this type of ministry yet. The fact that the definitions are so clearly descriptive provides us with an indisputable biblical validation for their use in these modern days.

Chapter 5
Banner
דֶּגֶל

"Raising the Standard"
39

Heavenly Impact

The words banners, flags and standards are used interchangeably throughout all modern translations of the Bible. Their basic meanings are the same.
Standard: Hebrew word: Degal #1714 daw-gal' to flaunt, a flag, banner, standard. Be conspicuous, chiefest.
Banner: #5251 Nace: a flag, a signal, sign, standard. From #5264 to gleam from afar. to be conspicuous as a signal to raise up a banner. *Heb./Greek Dictionary* A banner used at the top of a pole to mark a rallying point esp. in battle or to serve as an emblem. Something established by authority or custom or general consent. A cloth, usually bearing emblems or figures, born on a staff, and employed to distinguish one party or nationality from another. *Webster's Dictionary.*

Flag is a relatively modern word. The word flag used in Bible days meant weeds or rushes that grew along the water. Today it means a small banner; any size or shape of cloth attached a pole of some kind. The pole of the ancient standards were made up of a tree branch, as was the cross. Jesus spoke these words describing the manner Jesus would die (Lifted up on a tree).

1st.Peter 2:24 Who Himself bore our sins in His own body on the tree, that we, having died to sins, might live for righteousness--by whose stripes you were healed. NKJV.
We can parallel this lifting of the standard as a type of memorial to Jesus. Our declaration about Him is on the fabric at the top of the pole. He hung on a tree (pole) and died, in order that we might be saved and have eternal life. We don't usually think about this definition as we lift our banners in celebration.
The standard, banner or flag is composed of two elements. One is the fabric attached to the top of the pole and the other is the pole or stave known in Hebrew language as the Mat-teh', on which it is displayed. The definitions for the words flag or banner refers to the fabric (with the message displayed on it) not the pole.
I have heard some describe flags or banners as mat-teh's.
This could cause confusion for some people.

The Banner

The mat-teh' or the rod part of the banner (standard) does have its own particular significance, which is covered later.

Throughout the scripture we find that there were three main purposes for raising a physical standard or a banner which are still applicable today.

1. Banners were and still are used for the purpose of identification.

Numbers 2:2 The Israelites shall camp, each with standard, under the banners of their ancestral house; they shall camp around the Tent of Meeting at a distance. (Torah). Once again we see that each man was to have his own Mat-teh' with the banner attached to the top of it, to identify himself and his tribe. The twelve tribes were divided into four groups. One group or unit was on each side of the tabernacle. Each unit had their own banner, which distinguished their particular tribe.
The standard or Banner of Israel today bears the familiar Star of David. The blue stripes on it represent the stripes on the prayer shawl which is one of Israels' national religious symbols which stand as a memorial of God's covenant with the Jewish people and His land of Israel.

It is interesting that all nations even the ones shown to generally be pagan choose to identify themselves in this biblical way, each having their own particular flag.

We tend to think of banners as what we wave, not what we are. As imitators of Jesus we are considered to be a human display reflecting the message of Jesus and the Kingdom of God here on the earth, which is righteousness, peace and joy. Jesus was able to display these characteristics while he lived and moved amongst the people here on earth. People watch us, our actions speak louder than words. People will be drawn to this testimony of Christ-likeness that we portray as living banners for Him.

John 12:32 And I, if I be lifted up from the earth, I will draw all men unto me.

2 nd.Cor.3:2-3 But the only letter of recommendation we need is you yourselves! Your lives are a letter written in our hearts, and everyone can read it and recognize our good work among you. Clearly, you are a letter from Christ prepared by us. It is written not with pen and ink, but with the Spirit of the living God. It is carved not on stone, but on human hearts. NLT.
Matt.5:14-16 you are the light of the world--like a city on a mountain, glowing in the night for all to see. Don't hide your light under a basket! Instead, put it on a stand and let it shine for all. In the same way, let your good deeds shine out for all to see, so that everyone will praise your heavenly Father.NLT.

Banners are displayed to claim rulership or possession of a territory.

The majority of the scriptures containing the words standard or banner are military in description. *Num.2:10* says they set the standards according to their armies.
As we raise our standards and banners we are ...*as awesome as an army with banners! Song of Songs 6:4.*
This word picture presents a feeling of celebration at the site of an army advancing with their banners and flags waving! That is, if it is your army. Some translations use the word terrible instead of awesome when referring to banners. The root word for terrible is dreadful. To our spiritual enemies we cause a dreadful terror to come upon them as we raise our banners.
The translation of this scripture gives an explicit picture of what is happening in the spiritual realm as we lift these banners, a way to measure the impact we are making.
Isa.31:8-9 Then the Assyrian (enemy) shall fall by a sword not of man ;(the word of God), and a sword, not of men (but of God), shall devour him.

The Banner

And he shall flee from the sword, and his young men shall be subjected to forced labor. (In his flight) he shall pass beyond his rock (refuge and stronghold) because of terror; even his officers shall desert the standard in fear and panic, says the Lord, Whose fire is in Zion and Whose furnace is in Jerusalem. Amp.

As we apply the word of God to any area where the enemy has built a stronghold, a standard is raised, seen or unseen on earth, but visible in the heavenlies. The word which is our standard becomes a sword in the spirit which will strike terror in the heart of the enemy, he will flee in panic. Verse 9 states the enemy has a standard, one that he and his demons will quickly desert when the truth raises up. As we raise our banners they are a beacon of encouragement to those following behind and a message to those ahead, of who is coming forward to occupy and take possession of the land. To lift the banner of Jesus Christ is to say we are lifting up the word of God. This will cause great joy to the Lord. This is a safe platform from which to wage our war. The enemy has no defense against the word. He flees in terror at the word.
This is one of the ways we deal with spiritual strongholds in a spiritual way, which will produce a result in the physical realm.
Eph.6:12 for we do not wrestle against flesh and blood, but against principalities, against powers, against the rulers of the darkness of this age, against spiritual hosts of wickedness in the heavenly places.
For instance if a person had a stronghold of fear in their life and they begin to read the Bible and apply the word of God, in their life, faith will grow; as faith grows it becomes a standard. Faith is the opposite of fear. The enemy will desert his stronghold of fear and flee. He no longer will have the same influence on the person, he can't abide in the atmosphere of faith. This would pertain to any stronghold in a person's life. If the stronghold is lies, then when the standard of truth (the word of God) is raised lies will flee.

Heavenly Impact

This doesn't necessarily mean that the person is a liar, it could be that because of the lack or absence of truth he is able to be kept under bondage by lies that he hears in his head and believes about anything and everything.

The symbolic weapons the Lord gives us to use are a point of contact which serve to exercise and build our faith. As we receive more insight into the importance in the spiritual realm that these points of contact are and understand the language they speak, we will develop a greater sensitivity to the voice of God, which will ensure us the victory. Banners are a symbolic declaration of a proclamation concerning news, such as possessing the territory. *Jer.50:2 Proclaim and lift up a standard proclaim and do not conceal it.*

The Lord is telling Jeremiah to declare, publish and set up a standard (signal) to spread the news that the Lord has put the foreign gods of Babylon to shame and their idols are thrown down. This scripture projects the image of a warrior boldly planting a standard as a sign of taking possession of a territory. This banner becomes a signal, a testimony between the earth and the heavens. A visible sign.

As the banners of declaration and proclamation raise here in the physical earthly realm, there is an unseen gauntlet being thrown down in the spiritual realm.

Def. of gauntlet: challenge, symbol of war. *Webster's Dictionary.*
An Example; Remember watching shows about the settling of the west in America.

When an Indian warrior wanted to convey a message of possession of land or a symbol of impending war, he would raise his spear up in the air, give a shout then throw it down so it would stick into the ground.

Another example would be the pictures that show the American flag being planted in what had once been enemy territory by our service men. The way to possess the land usually entails a fight. Be prepared in an intercession setting, to praise and wave the banner until you spiritually have an inner peace that the mission is accomplished, and the victory won.

43

The Banner

Ps.20:5 We will rejoice in your salvation, and in the name of our God we will set up our banners! May the Lord fulfill all your petitions.

Jer 51:12 Set up the standard upon the walls of Babylon, make the watch strong, set up the watchmen, prepare the ambushes: for the LORD hath both devised and done that which he spake against the inhabitants of Babylon.

This would pertain to what is written on the banner you lift up in worship either in letter form or symbolism. We mustn't take spiritual victories for granted. Guard them. Make the watch strong, put them in place (intercessors), listening in the spirit for further instructions from our commander and chief (the Lord Sabboath.) We co-labor with the Lord in intercession. As we lift our standards declaring the word of the Lord as a prophetic proclamation the enemy will be defeated. We are informed of this parallel so that we may be spiritually prepared for the reaction to our action, and follow through accordingly.

In the spiritual realm as we lift our banners. We are as a strong people set in battle array.

Ps.60:4 Thou hast given a banner to them that fear thee, that it may be displayed because of the truth. Selah. Truth # 548 Heb /Greek something fixed, a covenant, a portion, sure.

When we see little orange flags sticking out of the ground it is a universal symbol that says, "Don't dig here!" These flags are a warning that something important and possibly hazardous to the digger is under those flags. We are tabernacles of God's presence, living banners. We show up in the spiritual kingdom as red flags. The enemy knows if he digs, there will be consequences. Not that this will stop him, but with knowledge of this concept we can be prepared.

Banners are used in celebration and as a symbol of the Lord's love and victory for His people.

Heavenly Impact

The earliest example of the use of the banner is in Ex. 17:15. Moses celebrated a victory over the Amalekites by building an alter, calling the name of it Jehovah Nissi which means, "The Lord is my banner."

Ex.17:15 And Moses built an altar, and called the name of it Jehovah-nissi; Hebrew -Jehovah -Yahweh-Jesus Nissi: banner, signal. "Jesus is my banner" As we raise our flags and banners we are symbolically exalting the name of the Lord, as Moses did. This truth is an eternal message, not just for Old Testament covenant people, but relevant for us today.

Alters were built of stones. The Bible calls us living stones. We become the physical alter to the Lord with our banners raised proclaiming Jehovah Nissi.

1st. Peter 2:5 Ye also, as lively stones, are built up a spiritual house, an holy priesthood, to offer up spiritual sacrifices, acceptable to God by Jesus Christ.

Song of songs. 2:4 He brought me to the banqueting house, and his banner over me was love.

Zach.9:16 The Lord their God will save them in that day, as the flock of His people. For they shall be like the jewels of a crown, lifted like a banner over His land.

The Lord has a banner. His name is Jesus!

Is.11:12 And in that day there shall be a Root of Jesse, who shall stand as a banner to the people; for the Gentiles shall seek Him, and His resting place shall be glorious.

This scripture speaks of Gentile believers, those who are not Jews by bloodline, but Gentiles who have been adopted into the family of God because they believe in Yeshua.

As we read on we see that the Lord has given written instructions in His word concerning believing Gentiles and the part they are to play in restoring God's chosen people (the Jews) back to the land of Israel thus fulfilling end-time prophecy before the return of the Lord.

The Banner

Is.62:10 Go out! Prepare the highway for my people to return! Smooth out the road; pull out the boulders; raise a flag for all the nations to see. NLT.
Is.49:22 Thus saith the Lord God: "Behold, I will lift up mine hand to the Gentiles, and set up my standard to the people: and they shall bring thy sons in their arms, and thy daughters shall be carried upon their shoulders."

Universal symbolism of the flag.

 There is a universal unspoken symbolic language of the standard. In any country when the flag is flying high all is well. If there is a message of tragedy or death it will fly at half-mast. The flag flying upside down is a sign of distress. This is a universal unspoken language throughout the world.
There is a positive effect on our physical body when we wave a banner. Our physical body rises; it has to respond in some way. It is hard to wave a flag sitting down. Even if we are sitting down, our arms raise up.
As we are proclaiming that Jesus Christ is the standard over our lives, we are presenting an outward display of our inward convictions. Our spirit man rises, our soul nature; mind, will and emotions, come into agreement with the spirit of God.
We become united, spirit, soul, and body. This is our proper position for victory.
This is one of the first visible signs that we are becoming an army.

Another style of flag.

Most of us are familiar with the rectangular shaped flags which come in all sizes. There is another style of flag that is fast becoming popular. It is generally called a wing flag. Each flag is a semi-circle. This shape resembles a wing. These flags are quite beautiful when they are used in worship especially with one in each hand. They remind us of the angels and the winged creatures in the throne room waving their wings and crying "Holy is the Lord." *Rev. 4:8.*

" Throne-room wing flags"

Ps. 36:7 How excellent is thy lovingkindness, O God! therefore the children of men put their trust under the shadow of thy wings.
Ps. 63:7 Because thou hast been my help, therefore in the shadow of thy wings will I rejoice.
Isa. 40:31 But they that wait upon the LORD shall renew their strength; they shall mount up with wings as eagles; they shall run, and not be weary; and they shall walk, and not faint.
We call this style "Throne room wing flags." We want to place our attention on the throne and the one seated upon it.

Symbolic Movements

These movements are just a few examples that can be made with the flags.
"Opening the Heavens"

 Hold the bottom of the pole of your flag or banner and make a large circle above your head in a clockwise, horizontal direction so the flag is flowing in a large circle above your head.
 Begin to turn in a circle in the same direction that the flag is traveling as you do this. As you are slowly turning in a circle (don't get dizzy) and making this movement you are symbolically opening the heavens, creating a portal above the worship, inviting the Spirit of the Lord to come into the midst of His people.

The Banner

"Holy Spirit descending into our midst."

(The flag can flow right into this movement from the opening of the heavens movement easily). If your flag is on a swing pole(slides around the shaft) circle up above the head then circle down below the waist. Repeat this while standing straight forward or moving in a circle. This can symbolize the Holy Spirit descending into your immediate sphere of influence bringing with him the fire of God into our midst.

"Butterfly Flourish."

Wave the flag in a circle eight movement. You can use two flags at once for this movement also. One flag wold follow after the other in the motion or you can spread your hands apart and cross over each other moving back and forth.
This symbolizes that there is always new-life in Christ. Life in Christ is a continuous changing
pattern, which will never end. You can perform this continuous movement in front of you or at the sides, as you spin the flag around in a circle or above your head.

"Fan the Flame"

Move the flags back and forth in a fanning movement, in any direction
2 Tim.1:6 This is why I remind you to fan into flames the spiritual gift God gave you when I laid my hands on you. New Living Translation © 1996 Tyndale Charitable Trust

48

Heavenly Impact

"From God's heart to our hands"

When you have different people in praise, worship and intercession each performing the same movement with the different instruments, in one location we see the scripture says this can be a very powerful tool to be used.

Matt.18:19 Again I say unto you, That if two of you shall agree on earth as touching any thing that they shall ask, it shall be done for them of my Father which is in heaven.

Chapter 6
The Shofar
שׁוֹפָר

"The Shout of the Lord"

Heavenly Impact

The ancient sound of the shofar is once again being heard throughout the nations. Its testimony echoes across the centuries, bridging the divide separating us from the Hebrew children, who witnessed the First Great Trump, the sound of the shofar of God at Mt.Sinai. (*Ex.19:16.*) This sound is timeless, it means the same now as it did then, the signal of Gods presence, sounding a divine, eternal, inspirational message which declares to the heaven and the earth:

The King is coming in Power and Glory!

1st.Thes. 4:16 For the Lord Himself will descend from heaven with a shout, with the voice of an archangel, and with the shofar of God. And the dead in Christ will rise first. PNT.

The shofar is mentioned over 80 times in the Bible as a ram's horn, trumpet or silver trumpet. Most modern translations use these words interchangeably throughout scripture.
However, there is a difference between them. The shofar most commonly used in biblical times came from either a domesticated ram or the wild Ibex goat. (Def. of Ibex: any of several wild goats, living chiefly in high mountain areas of the Old World and having large recurved horns transversely ridged in front).
Their horns could grow up to 56 inches in length forming a semi-circle over their backs. They are almost extinct. *Encyclopedia Britannica*. The ref. to these Ibex are found in Ps.104:18, 1st. Sam.24:2 and Job 39:1.
The shofars that replaced the rare Ibex are called Yemenite horns. They differ from the ram's horns in their long length, and multiple twistings. They are taken from the African antelope called the Kudu.

Definitions of the word Shofar/Trumpet

In the New Testament, the Greek text uses the same word, Salpiggi for both trumpet and shofar.

51

The Shofar

Most references to the trumpet in the New Testament speak of the return of the Messiah. (The word trumpet has the root word shofar.) We see this confirmation through the prophet Isaiah who writes of the day when the Messiah shall return with the sound of the great trumpet. *Isaiah 27:13 And it shall come to pass in that day, that the great <u>trumpet</u> (# 7782-showphar), shall be blown, and they shall come which were ready to perish in the land of Assyria, and the outcasts in the land of Egypt, and shall worship the LORD in the holy mount at Jerusalem.*

With the permission of Bill Morford the author of the *Power New Testament,* which I am using as the New Testament reference Bible throughout this book, I have inserted the word shofar for the word trumpet when the word refers back to the number in the Strongs Concordance for the word shofar.

In use today are two basic types of shofars: The Yemenite shofar and the Rams horn. I have heard the Yemenite which is the larger, longer shofar is also called a celebration shofar.

According to Mr. Morford concerning this issue of two shofars used for different reasons: "Although certain groups may prefer different uses, those are not defined in the Talmud or other ancient sources. The Yemenite is just fancier. Any shofar works as a call to repentance, there is no differing regarding the occasion." The Yemenite is the popular shofar blown at Jewish celebrations and certain feasts such as Rosh Hashanah the Jewish New Year, "Rosh" means "head" and "Shanah" means "year" in Hebrew. Blown at this time to praise the GOD of Israel for His blessing that will be placed upon the New Year.

This shofar is blown along with the silver trumpets, which will be covered later in the chapter.
Lev.25: 9-10: Then shalt thou cause the <u>trumpet</u> <u>of the jubilee</u> (celebration) to sound on the tenth day of the seventh month.

Heavenly Impact

The shofar was sounded as an instrument of proclamation, to sound an alarm, to assemble the people for solemn assembly (repentance) and worship; and to usher in the high holy days and feasts. *Webster's seventh New Collegiate Dictionary.* In synagogues at the conclusion of Yom Kippur, which is a high holy holiday of Jewish national and personal repentance of sin before God, the ram's horn is blown. Kippur is the Hebrew word Kapper, "To Cover." According to this meaning, symbolically God covers the sins of His people by the blood of the sacrifice.

The usual horn blown is the smaller ram's horn, also known as the horn of repentance. It is called this because as the Hebrew children blew on the ram's horn, they were usually singing about the mercy of the Lord upon them as a nation, because they were assembled in an attitude of repentance before Him.

Lev.23:27Also on the tenth day of this seventh month there shall be a day of atonement: it shall be a holy convocation unto you; and ye shall afflict your souls, and offer an offering made by fire unto the LORD .KJV. Num.29:28 (A ram slain for a sin offering.)

Shofar # 7782 Hebrew sho-far': a curved ram's horn. Cornet. (As giving a clear sound, in the original sense of incising, meaning to cut through.)

Trumpet: #2689 khats-o-tser-aw a trumpet. #4536(Greek) trump; quavering or reverberation a trumpet, from # 4525 a vibration, wave, billow.

The voice of the Shofar

As we study the scriptures pertaining to the shofar we see that the Lord chooses to represent His own voice with the sound of the Shofar.

Rev.1:10 I was in the Spirit on the Lord's day, and heard behind me a great voice, as of a shofar, saying, I am Alpha and Omega, the first and the last: and, What thou seest, write in a book, and send it unto the seven churches which are in Asia; unto Eph'-e- sus,

and unto Smyrna, and unto Per'-ga-mos, and unto Thy-a-ti'ra, and
unto Sar'-dis, and unto Philadelphia, and unto La-od-i-ce'a.
P.N.T.
Rev.4:1 after this I looked, and behold, a door was opened in
heaven: and the first voice which I heard was as it were of a shofar
talking with me: which said, Come up hither, and I will shew thee
things which must be hereafter. P.N.T.

Powerful characteristics of the voice of the Lord exhibited through the sound of the shofar!

Ex.19:16-19 on the morning of the third day, there was thunder,
lightning and a thick cloud on the mountain. Then a shofar blast
sounded so loudly that all the people in the camp trembled. Moshe
brought the people out of the camp to meet God; they stood near the
base of the mountain. Mount Sinai was enveloped in smoke,
because Adonai descended onto it in fire -its smoke went up like the
smoke from a furnace, and the whole mountain shook violently. As
the sound of the shofar grew louder and louder, Moshe spoke and
God answered him with a voice. Complete Jewish Bible
Scriptures that speak of the voice of the Lord usually include
mention of a mighty vibration.
Shofar #4536 salpigx {sal'-pinx} (Greek) trump; #4535 a
vibration, wave, billow.
Ex 20:18-19 all the people experienced the thunder, the lightning,
the sound of the shofar, and the mountain smoking.
When the people saw it, they tremble. Standing at a distance, they
said to Moshe," you speak with us; and we will listen. But don't let
God speak with us, or we will die." Complete Jewish Bible.

According to the Torah commentary the sound was so
penetrating that the people could actually "see the sounds" If the
Lord hadn't stopped the loud sound when he did the people may
have literally vibrated apart.

54

Heavenly Impact

Vibrations from sound waves have been a source of interest for scientists for years. Science says certain pitches or tones (vibrations) of sound waves can cause great confusion in the mind of people or animals that are within the range of these sound waves. They have other strong side effects, which could render an enemy helpless without firing a shot.
This has to do with the strength of vibration focused on a target. Some sound waves can be heard in the natural, but not necessarily. They can be powerful enough to cause an explosion, even within a person or object.

The Lord is the creator of the universe. When He speaks all creation trembles and vibrates. He can focus these waves where He wants to for His purposes.

Isa.29:6 Thou shalt be visited of the Lord of hosts with thunder, and with earthquake, and great noise, with storm and tempest, and the flame of devouring fire. For our God is a consuming fire.
Rev.11:19 and the temple of God was opened in heaven, and there was seen in his temple the ark of his testament: and there were lightenings, and voices, and thunderings, and an earthquake, and great hail.

In the story of Gideon and his men found in Judges chapters 6 and 7 it is not beyond the realm of possibility that when the men blew on their ram's horns, symbolic of the voice of the Lord, and broke the pitchers covering the lamps, symbolizing the Father of lights coming into their midst, there was so much noise, (vibrations targeted at the Midianites) in the spiritual realm that it terrorized the enemy into a chaos and panic.
They declared with a shout the prophetic word that the Lord had given Gideon in chapter 7 verse 9: The sword of the Lord (the divine-heavenly), and of Gideon (humanity-earthly), were in unity, to defeat their enemies.

55

The Shofar

In this great spiritual battle Gideon's 300 men stood their ground against 135,000 Midianites. We see the proof that the Lord was helping Gideon in this revelatory scripture.

Judges 6:34 But the Spirit of the LORD came upon Gideon, and he blew a trumpet; and Abiezer was gathered after him. Abiezer#44 in the Hebrew Greek; Father of helps.

Zech.9:14 Adonai will appear over them, and his arrow will flash like lightning. Adonai Elohim will blow the shofar and go out in the whirlwinds of the south. Complete Jewish Bible.

Why do we blow with the shofar of a ram?

As we call out to the Lord via the ram's horn shofar He will remember the binding of Isaac, and the ram that was sacrificed on the alter in his place. A ram that the Lord provided in His grace and mercy to take the place of Isaac.
The sound of the blowing of the ram's horn to the ears of the Lord, it is as if we have bound ourselves to His alter.
As we blow on the shofar we are making a declaration of supernatural intervention and provision. This sound serves as a perpetual reminder of God's faithfulness. God is aroused by the sound of the shofar to bless His people with His presence and His help.

Symbolism of the Horn

Horns are a symbol of governmental authority throughout scripture. Both in the earthly setting and the heavenly realm.
Dan.7:24 And the ten horns out of this kingdom are ten kings that shall arise: and another shall rise after them; and he shall be diverse from the first, and he shall subdue three kings.

Heavenly Impact

Because of the symbolism of the shofar it must come from the correct God approved source and be processed in a certain God approved way before using it to represent His voice and His authority on the earth.

This biblical trumpet, or shofar, when processed correctly is made from the hollowed out horn of a kosher animal, one which chews the cud and has cloven hooves. In the Jewish mindset this means that it is hollow so that the breath of HaShem or Adonai, God Himself would fill it and cause us to hear. The exception to this kosher rule would be the horn of a cow. This type of horn is never used because the Jewish people fear that they may remind God of the time the Hebrew children sinned by making a golden calf as an idol. *Ex.32:8.* They would not dare introduce an accuser where they need a defender. We, as Believers also need to have an understanding of this revelation, before presumptuously blowing on a shofar.

 We need to examine ourselves for any idols in our lives before blowing on the shofar. When we hear the shofar we are to remember our need to repent, to make a deliberate choice to bind ourselves spiritually to God's alter in deep heartfelt repentance of sin.
Interestingly enough, through the ages, one of the trademark emblems of the adversary/accuser has been the set of horns that is usually pictured on his head to symbolize his authority. Historically they have been the horns of a cow. They accurately represent that he is a counterfeit. The blowing of a cow's horn will draw attention in the spiritual realm, but not the type of attention a child of the Most High God would desire.
The trumpet (shofar) was blown at the de-throning, or de-horning of evil powers. 2nd.kings 11:14-18. The shofar blown as a tribute unto the Lord of Hosts proclaiming a victory over evil. *2 Sam.20:22-25.*

The Shofar

The enemy has been given a certain amount of authority
to invade our lives, for the purposes of God. We see this in Job
and many other places in the scripture. God's ways are higher
than our ways. We trust the Lord. We don't want to give satan a
license to any more entrance into our lives than what the Lord
allows for our refining. It is our job to de-horn the accuser in the
areas of our lives that he tries to horn into.

*Joel 2:12 "Now, therefore, says the Lord, turn to me with all your
heart, with fasting, with weeping, and with mourning. So rend
your heart, and not your garments; Return to the Lord your
God, for He is gracious and merciful, Slow to anger, and of great
kindness; And He relents from doing harm."*
As believers blowing on the shofar, we are symbolically
proclaiming the Government of God, over ourselves and over our
land. When we live in a state of humility, obedience and
reverence before the Lord we are effectively de-horning satan.
We are removing his authority over our lives.
*Joel 2:1,12: -13 Blow the shofar in Zion, and sound an alarm in
My holy mountain! Let all the inhabitants of the land tremble; for
the day of the Lord is coming, for it is at hand:*

When the Lord spoke to Abraham at the binding of Isaac He
intervened in Grace and Mercy. When He returns it will be in
Judgment. We need this reminder to be repentant in attitude
before the Lord at all times. Crying out like the Hebrew children
before their enemies. His mercy and Grace endure forever!

Physical parallels between the shofar and us.

We are to remind ourselves at the blowing of the shofar, of the
Lord's work in us, which parallels the preparation of the shofar
to be fit for His use. The shofar is a vessel made up of bone and
cartilage with blood flowing through it.

Heavenly Impact

It has to be taken from a live animal which requires a sacrifice. The horn has to be cleaned on the inside much like we do. This is done with heat. The cartilage is stripped out. This would be our equivalent of being tested by fire; this fire process is necessary to elicit a transformation within ourselves.

These great fiery trials of faith should be more precious than gold to us, they are how we mature spiritually.
God uses multiple means to prepare us to be fit for our destiny. He knows the best way to clean out our fleshly natures.

While the shofar is still hot, the mouthpiece may be cut and formed while it is still bendable.
Jewish tradition says the curve of the shofar, especially the single bend of the short shofar, reflects the bending of our will in submission to the Almighty. It is curved, as if pointing the way back to God. It is this bent shofar instead of a straight trumpet that is used to signal repentance and humility.

To repent in many biblical passages is "SHUVAH," which means literally "turn," or "return." A portion read on Shabbat Shuvah, the Shabbat of repentance between Rosh Hashanah and Yom Kippur;
*Hosea 14:2-9. It begins: O Israel, return (shuvah) to the Lord your God, for you have stumbled because of your iniquity; take words with you and return (shuvu) to the Lord. Say to Him "Take away all iniquity; receive us graciously, for we will offer the sacrifices of our lips." (*Praise.)
Lastly the outside of the shofar is polished. Our human flesh nature says polish up the outside first. We might fool man this way, but not the Lord. He looks upon the inner man.
Either the Yemenite shofar or the ram's horn might be polished or might be left in the rough state.

The Shofar

Silver trumpets

There are several passages in the word which speak specifically about silver trumpets. The translation I will be using for the Old Testament scripture and additional commentary concerning the silver trumpets is from the *Jewish Chumash the Stone Edition copyright 1993, 1994, and 2000.* It gives a clearer, concise description of the trumpet signals.

Trumpet# 3104 in the Hebrew /Greek concordance. yov-ale' the blast of a horn. The signal of the silver trumpets: hence the instrument and the festival thus introduced: -Jubilee, rams horn, trumpet. #2689 chatsar {khaw-tsar'}) to sound a trumpet.
The silver trumpet was originally made for the Tabernacle of Moses, a straight instrument made of hammered silver with a flared end and no valves; traditionally it was blown only by the Levite priests. These trumpets were used as a signaling instrument, to summon the congregation, for breaking camp, to sound the alarm when
the people went to war, sounded in victory after battle, in religious ceremonies, and at feasts.

Today both the shofar (Yemenite) and the silver trumpet are used together in festivities such as Rosh Hashana, the Jewish New Year. On Yom Kippur, the national day of repentance, the smaller ram's horn is usually blown.
Num.10:1 HASHEM (God) spoke to Moses, saying, Make for yourself two silver trumpets-make them hammered out, and they shall be yours for the summoning of the assembly and to cause the camps to journey.
Who was to sound these silver trumpets?
Num.10: 8 The sons of Aaron, the Kohanim (priests- Levites), shall sound the trumpets, and it shall be for you an eternal decree for your generations. Eternal: everlasting. *Webster's Dictionary.*

<u>Traditional</u> <u>Trumpet</u> <u>calls</u>.

Num.10:4 If they sound a long blast with one, the leaders shall assemble to you, the heads of Israel's thousands.

1. **The <u>Tekiah</u>** (the blast), one long blast with a clear tone. Such a blast from a single trumpet summoned the leaders to come together.
Num.10:3 When they sound a long blast with them, the entire assembly shall assemble to you, to the entrance of the tent of meeting.
This is an unbroken sound that calls the individual man and leadership to search his heart, abandon his evil ways, and seek forgiveness through repentance.

2. **The <u>Teruah</u>:** a rapid series of nine or more very short notes. This was a type of alarm, the signal to move out!
Num.10:5 When you sound short blasts the camp resting to the east shall journey. When you sound short blasts a second time, the camps resting to the south shall journey: short blasts shall they sound for their journey. When you gather together the congregation, you shall sound a long blast, but not a short blast.
Num.10:9 When you go to wage war in your land against an enemy who oppresses you, you shall sound short blasts of the trumpets, and you shall be recalled before HASHEM, your God, and you shall be saved from your foes.
When both trumpets sound the short blasts it is possible that the first trumpet is the signal for man (physical) (silver trumpets made by man) and the second is the signal for the heavenly (spiritual) creation to respond. (Shofar created by God) Today these 9 short blasts could be a prophetic signal that the Lord is about to move you or people being prayed for into a new spiritual / physical dimension.

The Shofar

3. The <u>Shevarim</u>: A broken, sighing sound of three short calls. It is a broken staccato, trembling sound. It typifies the sorrow that comes to a man when he realizes his wrong and desires to change his ways.

4. The <u>Tekiah</u> <u>Gedolah</u>: The great Tekiah, a single unbroken blast, held as long as possible, giving one and all the chance to repent and be reconciled to the Lord before His victorious return. It is this last blast that is referred to as the last trump.

The sound of the Shofar grips our spirit, "Wake up sleeper! Hear the voice of the Lord! He is coming. Prepare your heart. Repent, turn away from all sin and disobedience."

<u>These</u> <u>ancient</u> <u>trumpet</u> <u>signals</u> <u>are</u> <u>used</u> <u>today.</u>

Num.29:1 And in the seventh month, on the first day of the month, ye shall have a holy convocation; ye shall do no servile work: it is a day of blowing the trumpets unto you.

The sounding of the Shofar is commanded particularly for the holiday of Rosh Hashanah, which is also called Yom Teruah, The Day of Sounding the Shofar. Yom means Day, Teruah means to blow the trumpet or sound alarm. Before sounding the shofar, the blower recites the following two blessings:

1. Blessed are You, Adonai our God, King of the universe, who sanctified us with His commandments and commanded us to hear the sound of the shofar.
2. Blessed are You, Adonai our God, King of the universe, who kept us in life and sustained us and allowed us to reach this season. The congregation responds with "Amen."

As New Covenant believers, we are considered to be priests unto the Lord. This gives us legal spiritual right to be blowing the shofars or the silver trumpets.

Heavenly Impact

1st.Peter 2:9 We are a chosen generation, a royal priesthood, and holy nation, a peculiar people; that ye should shew forth the praises of him who hath called you out of darkness into His marvelous light.
Rev.1:5-6; And from Jesus Christ, who is the faithful witness, and the first begotten of the dead, and the prince of the kings of the earth. Unto him that loved us, and washed us from our sins in His own blood. And hath made us kings and priests unto God and His father; to him be glory and dominion for ever and ever A-men.

These ancient calls are applicable today. As we blow the trumpets or shofar's in faith, fully believing that we are activating a response in the spiritual realm which will make a difference in our physical realm, we ought to study the correct calls, to prevent spiritual confusion
Military trumpeters blow certain calls on their trumpets; it could be compared to a type of Morse code, which provides a medium of exchange of information without a word being spoken.

1 Cor.14:7-8 And even things without life giving sound, whether pipe or harp, except they give a distinction in the sounds, how shall it be known what is piped or harped? For if the trumpet give an uncertain sound, who shall prepare himself to the battle.

The shofar blown during intercession.

The word gives us many references where the shofar was blown in a military, warfare setting, the sound of the shofar announcing the manifested presence of the commander and chief coming on the scene himself. As we embrace and encourage the use of the shofar during times of intercession, we are reminding the Lord as well as ourselves, that He is the one who wins our battles, when we are obedient to His commandments.

The Shofar

Numbers 10:9 And if ye go to war in your land against the enemy that oppresseth you, then ye shall blow an alarm with the trumpets; and ye shall be remembered before the Lord your God, and ye shall be saved from your enemies.

"In your land" can mean physical description of a geographical area or it can mean your own life and personal circumstances.

Joshua 6:13-20 And seven priests bearing seven trumpets of ram' horns before the ark of the Lord went on continually, and blew with the shofars: and the armed men went before them; but the rearguard came after the ark of the Lord, the priests going on, and blowing with the shofars. On the second day they compassed the city enclosure once and returned to the camp. So they did for six days. On the seventh day they rose early at daybreak and marched around the city as usual, only on that day they compassed the city seven times. And the seventh time, when the priests had blown the shofars, Joshua said to the people, "Shout! For the Lord has given you the city." So the people shouted when the priests blew with the shofars;(ram's horns); and it came to pass, when the people heard the sound of the shofar, and the people shouted with a great shout, that the wall fell down flat, so that the people went up into the city, every man straight before him, and they took the city. CJB. This blast of the ram's horn is music to the ears of the Lord!

Ps.47:5 God goes up to shouts of acclaim, Adonai to a blast on the shofar. Complete Jewish Bible.
To the Canaanites this was a strange way of fighting -marching around in silence except for the blowing of the shofars', there was no effort to scale the wall, no weapons were used, no engines of siege were brought up, and no other ordinary means of warfare were used in any degree.
 The sight of armed men marching day after day, seven times; the seventh day must have been a merry making spectacle to the inhabitants of Jericho.

Heavenly Impact

They had never seen or heard of such a seemingly foolish thing, and neither had the Israelites, but they were in strict obedience to one who takes the foolish things to confound the wise and the weak things to destroy the mighty. *Dake's Annotated ref. Bible.* The Lord expects us to co-labor with him. He and the heavenly host do the actual physical fighting, it is our part to speak or sing the word of God concerning the battle and praise the Lord for the victory!

2nd. Chron.20:22 Now when they began to sing and to praise, the Lord set ambushes against the people of Ammon, Moab, and Mount Seir, who had come against Judah, and they were defeated. SFLB. 2nd. Chron.20:28-29 So they came to Jerusalem, with stringed instruments, and harps and trumpets (shofars), to the house of the Lord. And the fear of God was on all the kingdoms of those countries when they heard that the Lord had fought against the enemies of Israel. SFLB.

Israel became a nation on May 14, 1948. The rebuilding began in both the physical and spiritual realm for the nation.

This Jewish nation is preparing for their King, the Messiah, to come and take his place in Jerusalem. Jewish tradition says the Messiah will come during the festival of the Feast of Tabernacles.

Amos 9:11 In that day will I raise up the tabernacle (sukkah-booth, referring to David's lineage) of David that is fallen, and close up the breaches thereof; and I will build it up as in the days of old. That they may possess the remnant of Edom, and of all the heathen, (gentiles) which are called by my name, saith the Lord that doeth this.

Many believe that this Tabernacle of David is the 24 hour houses of prayer and praise now springing up throughout the nations, singing and declaring the word of the Lord, which will encompass the Davidic physical style of worship with flags, tabrets, shofars, streamers and other symbolic biblical worship and praise adornment items.

The Shofar

As we are in the preparation of the rebuilding of the Tabernacle of David it is significant to note that David was anointed with a shofar of oil.

1st.Sam.16:13 Then Samuel took the horn of oil and anointed him in the midst of his brothers; and the Spirit of the Lord came upon David from that day forward. So Samuel arose and went to Ramah.

The difference in this use of the shofar filled with oil is found in *1st.sam.16: 1 "The Lord said to Samuel, How long will you mourn for Saul, seeing I have rejected him from reigning over Israel? Fill your horn with oil: I will send you to Jesse the Bethlehemite. <u>For I have provided for Myself</u> a king among his sons."*

King David was to be different. He would serve the nation, but he was to be set aside to minister praise and worship unto the Lord. The anointing with the oil of the shofar symbolized God's presence in authority and power, manifesting especially during times of praise and worship.
The commissioning with the oil from a shofar appears to be a special commissioning into a ministry that could be called The Royal priesthood of highly anointed praise and worship. There are shofars that can be purchased for this specific purpose which have leather on one end and a type of cork in the other end.

The person who is conducting the commissioning would usually pour the oil out of the shofar and over the person's head as he is consecrated. It should be poured on the crown of the head, according to Jewish tradition. The crown of the head means the highest point, ruler, top.
 Another interesting aspect of the use of the oil in the shofar would be to anoint the end of the shofar, or pour some consecration oil into your shofar and blow it.

Heavenly Impact

This particular oil (*Ex.30.*) has a high vibration due to the pure plant matter it is composed of (if made correctly) along with the olive oil. It will magnify your proclamation that your are set apart for the Lord's service across the heavenlies as you blow it after applying the oil.

There was one other recorded in the word who was anointed in this way. It was King David's son, Solomon, who built the temple as a resting place for the presence of the Lord.
1st.king 1:39 Then Zadok the priest took a horn of oil from the tabernacle and anointed Solomon. And they blew the horn, and all the people said, "Long live King Solomon!"

Symbolic Movement

The following is a testimony given by a friend concerning the sounding of the shofar prophetically in a prayer meeting in a nearby city.
I was asked to blow the shofar at the start of the meeting. I asked the Holy Spirit to lead me in the blowing because I don't have knowledge of the proper calls. The first time I blew a long blow without a break in it. I did this a couple of times.

" Next, I blew three short blasts while turning in a circle. I did this until I had made several circles. The strange thing was, as I was turning in the circles the shofar began to move up and down like a wave, like it had a life of its own."
" Lastly I began to blow a great long sound. It was almost as if I had more air in my lungs than ever before. The sound went on much longer than the first long blow. I don't understand what the calls meant, but knew that things were really happening in the spiritual realm as I blew."
I believe the Lord was using the Breath of the Holy Spirit, blown through the vehicle of the shofar, to speak symbolically to the people the following interpretation.

The Shofar

The first call sounds like this person was blowing the Tekiah signal. This is an unbroken sound that calls the individual man and leadership to search his heart, abandon his evil ways, and seek forgiveness through repentance. The people in this meeting were corporately united, praying a prayer of repentance on behalf of themselves, their leaders and the leadership of the city, before moving on to other business.

This is our personal responsibility before entering into the presence of God. Sometimes we are presumptuous and blast right into His Holy presence before the preparation of cleansing ourselves spiritually.

Our goal is to acknowledge His awesome Holiness and our respect for it. By blowing twice, simulating two shofars, or if there were more shofars each blowing this same long blast, it would mean a call to the people to come together to the entrance of the sanctuary in corporate unity.

The three short blasts: The Shevarim: A broken, sighing sound of three short calls. It is a broken staccato, trembling sound. It typifies the sorrow that comes to a man when he realizes his wrong and desires to change his ways.

The Torah commentary says: When you go to wage war in your land, the shofars be sounded to arouse the congregation. The torah commands that whenever the land is struck by distress, whether it is war, epidemic, or drought, these blasts are a call to repentance, and a reminder that distress is a product of sin.

For people to interpret such problems as merely coincidental is cruel, because this will prevent the nation from changing its ways and cause them to continue the corrupt practices that caused misfortune to befall them in the first place.

Heavenly Impact

Turning in the circle while blowing the shofar could mean many things. One example could be that the Lord is going to come into our midst as a whirlwind and turn things around. If He comes as a whirlwind he will certainly blow things around!
Whirlwind: a forward-moving current of air whirling violently in a vertical spiral. Webster's Dictionary.

Zech.9:14 And the Lord shall be seen over them, and his arrow shall go forth as the lightning: and the Lord God shall blow the shofar, and shall go with the whirlwinds of the south.

The person who blew the shofar said that she and others in the meeting discerned that it symbolized the stirring up and the calling forth of the gifts of the Holy Spirit.
The wavy movement could be an interpretation of a symbolic wave offering before the Lord in the format of sound waves.

To dispel confusion about more than one person blowing the shofar in a meeting, I go back to the scripture in Numbers 10:9. It says when you go to wage war, which could mean prayerful intercession, it is important to pay attention to the protocol of the meeting concerning the blowing of the shofar. The leadership should designate a shofar player. If more than one, they should be in close contact with each other in the meeting or have a plan prearranged. We can see how more than one shofar blowing at random during intercession could bring confusion in the spiritual realm. Gideon told his men how and when to blow their ram's horns so they were in unity.

I know that at times of celebrations that many people are blowing shofars at the same time, with all different sounds.
There doesn't seem to be anywhere in the word of God that says there is anything wrong with this type of celebration blowing.

The Shofar

Another testimony:
A friend and her grandson were coming to visit me one evening. On the way she was explaining to him about blowing the shofar over the land announcing the presence of the Lord. She showed him how to blow it out the window while driving down the road. He took the shofar and put it out his window, pointed it upward and turned to ask her a question. When he did this the wind (breath of the Lord), blew back through the shofar into the car! It was awesome to hear the Lord respond. When they rushed in to tell me, we ran back out to the car and began to drive up and down blowing to the Lord and receiving back from Him!

Important reasons for blowing the shofar.

The Bible reveals the genuine strategic function of blowing the shofar at the beginning of praise, worship and intercession. It is listed as a first priority in a lot of the scriptures concerning its use in worship and praise.

Ps.150:3-6 Praise him with the sound of the shofar: praise him with the psaltery and harp. Praise him with the timbrel and dance: Praise him with stringed instruments and organs. Praise him upon the loud cymbals: praise him upon the high sounding cymbals. Let every thing that hath breath praise the Lord. Praise ye the Lord.

Ps.98:6 with trumpets and sound of shofar make a joyful noise before the Lord, the King.

2 Chron.5:13 It came even to pass, as the trumpeters and singers were as one, to make one sound to be heard in praising and thanking the Lord; and when they lifted up their voice with the trumpets and cymbals and instruments of musick, and praised the Lord, saying, For He is good; for his mercy endureth forever; That then the house was filled with a cloud, even the house of the Lord; so that the priests could not stand to minister by reason of the cloud: for the glory of the Lord had filled the house of God.

Ps. 47:1 Clap your hands, all you peoples! Shout to God with the voice of triumph! The word shout here is #7321 roo-ah one of the sounds of the shofar.

Ps.47:5 God has ascended with a shout, The LORD, with the sound of a trumpet. NASB. Could this mean that the Lord stands up from the throne when we blow the shofar? According to the *Strong's concordance* the word ascended means to lift oneself, to spring up. That gives us an amazing word picture.

The Shofar is blown by watchmen/intercessors to rally troops, to sound an alarm.

There is the ministry of the watchman/intercessor. The office of watchman/intercessor is strategic for protection of the sheep. These watchman or watchwoman (by Jewish law, women can blow the shofar), are anointed with discernment or spiritual insight. They actually open the door for the Lord to come in. The word watchman in most translations reads porter which is the Greek word. #2377 thuroros {thoo-ro-ros'} 1) a doorkeeper, porter, male or female.

John 10:2 But he who enters by the door is the shepherd of the sheep. The watchman opens the door for this man, and the sheep listen to his voice and heed it; and he calls his own sheep by name and brings (leads) them.
John 18:16 But Peter stood at the door outside. Then the other disciple, who was known to the high priest, went out and spoke to her who kept the door, and brought Peter in.
Watchmen are the spiritual lookouts and protectors of specific bodies of people. When a person is functioning in this ministry he or she is responsible to hear the voice of the Lord and open the door, to warn the people when the Lord is about to bring judgment, so they might have a chance to examine their hearts and repent. In the Old Testament the watchman would warn the people by the blowing of the shofar.

71

The Shofar

The people understood this type of symbolic language.
Ezek 33:6-7 But if the watchman see the sword come, and blow not the shofar, and the people be not warned: if the sword come and take away any person from among them, he is taken away in his iniquity; but his blood will I require at the watchman's hand. So thou son of man, I have set thee a watchman unto the house of Israel; therefore thou shalt hear the word at my mouth, and warn them for me. CJB.
Neh.4:18-20 As for the construction- workers, each one had his sword sheathed at his side; that is how they built. <u>The man to sound the alarm on the shofar stayed with me.</u> I said to the nobles, the leaders, and the rest of the people, this is a great work, and it is spread out; we are separated on the wall, one far from another. But wherever you are, when you hear the sound of the shofar, come to that place, to us. Our God will fight for us! CJB (Emphasis mine).

<u>Physical and spiritual impact of blowing the shofar</u>

When blown in faith, the shofar releases unlimited spiritual power in the invisible for accomplishing God's purposes. Some people give testimony of seeing bright rainbow like colors in the spirit during worship and praise. Science confirms this spiritual reality which is beyond our natural capability of sight.

Following is a very simplistic scientific explanation of the powerful visual presentation that is released into the spiritual realm as we blow the shofar. Earth's atmosphere is composed of matter which is electro-magnetically charged. As we blow on the shofar a wave of energy or vibration (sound waves) is projected into this electromagnetic field. As this energy encounters moisture molecules it reflects off them creating a prism of light. (Light rays). The intensity of these colors reflected depends on the frequency pitch or tone of the sound vibration. There are seven basic musical tones, which have their own distinct frequency

72

relating to color. There are 7 major colors in the light spectrum. In essence we are flashing forth a rainbow of color, a spectacular light show to the Lord.

As He hears the sound of the shofar echoing across the heavens, along with our worship, He is bound to be moved.

He looks down and sees the light and colors projecting up from the earth. He remembers His covenant with us.

There are two additional definitions for the shofar not mentioned earlier, but are relevant to this section.

Hebrew #8231 Sha-far' to glisten.

Horn: #7160: To push or gore. To shoot out horns; fig. rays, to shine. From# 7161 a horn as projecting, a ray of light.

Gen.9:12-13 And God said, "This is the token of the covenant which I make between me and you and every living creature that is with you, for perpetual generations. I do set my bow in the cloud, and it shall be for a token of a covenant between me and the earth." Ezekiel 1:28 As the appearance of the bow that is in the cloud in the day of rain, so was the appearance of the brightness round about. This was the appearance of the likeness of the glory of the LORD. And when I saw it, I fell upon my face, and I heard a voice of one that spoke."

Rainbow: an arc containing the colors of the spectrum, formed in the sky by the refraction, reflection and dispersion of light in rain or fog. *Webster's Dictionary.*

Looking once more at the definitions of the word shofar, they make perfect sense, when applied to the symbolism of sound, light and color.

#8237 shaf-roor' from# 8231-splendid, a tapestry or canopy-a royal pavilion in the original sense of incising, meaning to cut through.

Not only are we creating a glorious light show by our worship, but we are preparing a royal canopy, a special place to meet with the Lord. This canopy also forms a protective covering over us in the spiritual realm, as we blow on the shofar and it cuts through the demonic realm, the enemy can't discern the source, his emotion is panic. (*Underlined emphasis mine*).

Ps.27: 5 For in the time of trouble he shall hide me in his pavilion: in the secret of his tabernacle shall he hide me; he shall set me up upon a rock. KJV.

Ps.31:12 Thou shalt hide them in the secret of thy presence from the pride of man: thou shalt keep them secretly in a pavilion from the strife of tongues.

Job.36:27-29.For He draws up drops of water, which distill as rain from the mist, which the clouds drop down and pour abundantly on man. Indeed, can anyone understand the spreading of clouds, the thunder from His canopy? NKJV.

This gives new meaning to *Rev.4:1-3 After this I looked, and, behold, a door was opened in heaven: and the first voice which I heard was as it were of a trumpet talking with me; which said, Come up hither, and I will shew thee things which must be hereafter. And immediately I was in the spirit: and, behold, a throne was set in heaven, and one sat on the throne. And he that sat was to look upon like jasper and a sardus stone: and there was a rainbow round about the throne, in sight like unto an emerald. (Underlined emphasis mine)*
Our Lord is the King of kings; no other King in the universe has a people whose worship lifts up this spectacular type of banner. There is no doubt among the hosts of heaven, the identity of our King during this colorful visible display!
Isa.18:3 All you inhabitants of the world you who live on the earth: when a banner is hoisted on the mountain, look! When a shofar is blown, listen! CJB.
 Ps.97:3 Fire goes before Him and burns up His adversaries round about. Amp. Our worship here on earth elicits a genuine impact in the heavenlies and can help to turn our situations around.

Heavenly Impact

What a glorious site in the heavenlies! The angelic host coming with the Lord to rejoice with His people, while the host of darkness are fleeing desperately, to escape getting burnt up in the presence of the Lord.

To use atmospheric terminology; any stormy, dark and gloomy weather condition in the spiritual realm that effects us in the physical realm will be turned into favorable sunny conditions for us.

The information in this chapter concerning sound to light to color has been gathered from a variety of sources, science books and the Internet. Usually one sentence here, one sentence there to make it understandable to the everyday non-scientific person like myself. To reference the information to each specific source would be impossible. After compiling the information it was checked by physics major, who assured me it is correct. I am not claiming that it is 100% accurate, I have just composed scientific facts in the easiest to understand manner possible.

Shofar playing

Some helpful ideas on how to blow the shofar.
1. Look closely at the mouthpiece. Turn the shofar around until the thickest part of the mouthpiece is in the most upright position.
2. The correct way to blow, is to place the mouthpiece against the fleshy part to the left or to the right-whichever side feels more comfortable. Most people, when beginning place it in the middle of the lips.
3. Take a deep breath, tighten and buzz your lips. Once you have produced a note. Tighten your lips to get a higher note. To get a long sustained blast, you must learn to breathe deeply.

Methods to clean your shofar.
The reason that most shofars smell bad is that when they are cleaned at the factory they cannot remove all residues from the inside. This residue is sinew and flesh that is clinging in crevices.

The Shofar

As it decays it smells.
The simplest method is to brush out whatever residue can be reached in the shofar, with a bottlebrush or any other means you can think of. Pour enough hydrogen peroxide to fill half the horn with the mouthpiece plugged. Swirl it back and forth until the residue is bubbled out. Pour out the liquid and repeat if necessary. Eventually no more residue will come out.
Another method of cleaning was demonstrated on a video by Dick Reuben called *"Sound the Shofar."*

Step 1. Buy a "nerf" ball (soft and pliable), an ear plug (the squeeze and insert type available at most drug stores), some fish tank gravel (not sand and not very big) and some alcohol.
Step 2. Plug the mouthpiece with the earplug. Pour in enough gravel that it can be shaken easily. Plug the bell end with the nerf ball.
Step 3. Play the "maraca" (shake it hard!) for about 15 minutes.
Step 4. Pull out the nerf ball and empty out the gravel. Pour about a cup of alcohol in and replace the ball. Shake for about a minute.
Step 5. Pull out the ball. Pour out the alcohol. Remove the earplug. Let it dry. The alcohol should dry quickly. It should eliminate the smell and disinfect the horn.
DO NOT let any liquid stay in too long. If necessary use a mild bleach solution but realize it will take a few days for the chlorine smell to dissipate. You could also use witch hazel with spearmint but use it sparingly. Stubborn smells can also be eliminated with odor neutralizers.
At times we have used "Oxi-clean" or a similar product. Fill the horn half full of hot, but not boiling water. Put in the scoop of product and then shake the horn with both ends plugged.
If the mouthpiece opening is not large enough for the air to get through easily, buy a small round file and file it out carefully.

Heavenly Impact

If you do not have a shofar God has made a provision for you.

Isa.58:1 Shout out loud! Don't hold back! Raise your voice like a shofar! Proclaim to my people what rebels they are, to the house of Ya'akov (Israel) their sins. CJB.

Once again we see the cry of the shofar is a cry to repent. The sound of the shofar, when blown, emanates from the most innermost part of our human being. At this moment, as we blow the shofar it is a reminder to us and a memorial to the Lord.

We are saying symbolically that we stand before Him as living dust, empowered by divine breath, the Ruach HaKodesh (Holy Spirit), transforming us to accomplish His purposes for our lives.

The scriptures bear out the testimony for the shofar. It should be treated with honor and respect, used for God's purposes, not to be blown to draw attention to ourselves, or taken lightly, but to be used with wisdom.

77

Chapter 7
The Streamer
שׂבֹּר

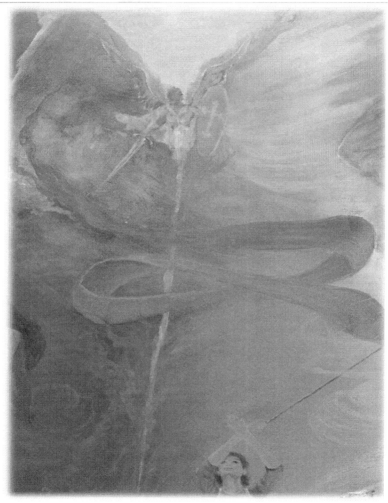

"Opening the Heavens"

Heavenly Impact

The streamer definitions in English and the Hebrew/Greek dictionary are very enlightening as to the purpose and function the streamer serves in the spiritual realm.

A streamer is a long tapering piece of fabric usually from 3-9 foot long, with a wooden dowel rod or a fiberglass handle on one end to hold onto. It can be wide or narrow like a ribbon. It will be made with a fabric that is light and airy, and flows smoothly.

Those of us who use the streamer have a sense in the spirit that when we use it in praise, worship and intercession that the heavens open. Now we have a way to gauge that fact according to the scripture.

Definition of the streamer

Streamer: Hebrew #7618: sh-buw {sheb-oo'} unused root word, through the idea of subdivision into flashes or streamers meaning as to flame. Identified with #7632 shabiyb {shaw-beeb'} - flame as to split into tongues-spark.

 This definition immediately brings to mind thoughts of the Holy Spirit manifesting upon the New Testament believers with tongues of fire, empowering them to do the work of the gospel. *Acts 2:2 When suddenly there came a sound from heaven like the mighty rushing <u>wind</u> and it filled the whole house in which they were sitting. And there appeared to them tongues resembling fire, which were separated and distributed, and that settled on each one of them. And they were all filled with the Holy Spirit and began to speak in other languages, as the <u>Spirit</u> kept giving them clear and loud expression (in each tongue, in appropriate words.)* Amplified Bible.
The words wind and spirit in this scripture refer back to #4154 wind, breath of life. a wind that is ethereal or divinely supernatural. To regenerate.

The Streamer

This divine wind brings the heavenly Host along to worship in our midst. *Ps.104:4 Who makes winds His messengers, flames of fire His ministers.*

We are His earthly messengers streaming forth this divine wind into our earthly setting. As we twirl and whirl we are enacting a picture of the Holy Spirit coming into our midst, settling on every person (with tongues of fire) distributing and filling each individually. Refreshing, liberating and motivating them to speak the word of God in boldness.

During the time of working on the scriptural validation for the streamer and the heavenly impact that is made when it is used, the Glorious Creations team went to Africa. While there I had a supernatural experience from the Lord which gave me an additional revelation about this instrument and some of its purposes. At first, you may not understand how the experience ties in with the definition of the streamer, but as you read along I think you will agree that it all fits together to paint the bigger picture.

While in Ghana, riding in the back seat of a car across the plains, the windows were down and the wind was blowing in my ears. I was looking out the window and praying in tongues, (*1.Cor. 12:9*) when suddenly the sound of the wind turned into tongues- many different individual languages. I listened attentively for a minute or two then asked the Lord for the interpretation. Each unknown tongue began to speak in English. They were all glorifying God with words of praise individually.

Some examples of what I heard are:

"Praise You Lord, creator of heaven and earth, maker of the universe I worship you!" Another was saying; "blessings and honor be unto Adoni the Lord God Most High!" It was like being in a room full of people and hearing different parts of conversations all praising and glorifying the Lord at the same time.

80

Heavenly Impact

I was thinking, this must be what the believers in the New testament experienced in the upper room when the Holy Spirit came in like the sound of a mighty wind. This sound is also described by John explaining his vision of heaven.

Rev.19:6-7 And I heard, as it were the voice of a great multitude, and as the voice of many waters, and even as the voice of many thunderings saying Alleluia, For the Lord God omnipotent reigneth. Let us be glad and rejoice, and give honor to him; for the marriage of the lamb is come, and His wife hath made herself ready.

Of course all wind is not necessarily from the Holy Spirit. The scriptures show us there is a parallel, a counterfeit. The wind can also have demonic forces behind it. We must have a word from the Holy Spirit discerning when to rebuke the demonic forces behind the wind in the name of Jesus.

Mk.4:39 And He (Jesus) arose, and rebuked the wind, and said unto the sea, Peace be still. And the wind ceased, and there was a great calm.

When we know the wind is of the Lord we can join in with
The heavenly host to worship God in unity.

In order to look at the streamer from a broader perspective concerning the impact made in the heavenly realm we see that streamer comes from the word stream: "A current of water, a steady flow that moves quickly. Pertaining to water or air."
Webster's New World Dictionary.

An example of a stream of air is the atmospheric condition called the jet stream. This is a fast moving stream or <u>current</u> <u>of wind.</u> Its action determines the weather in the upper realm of our hemisphere, affecting our weather upon the earth.

We want to make an impact spiritually on the atmospheric state in the heavenly realm through our worship, thus changing the physical condition on this earthly level where we are worshipping.

The Streamer

We see an example of the Lord using a human ambassador on the earth to change a weather pattern in the heavenlies to affect the earth through that person's worship.
1st. Kings 18:41-45. And Elijah said unto Ahab, Get thee up, eat and drink; for there is a sound of abundance of rain. So Ahab went up to eat and to drink. (Elijah made a prophetic statement.) *And Elijah went up to the top of Carmel; and he cast himself down upon the earth, and put his face between his knees,*
(Elijah worshipped the Lord.) Worship #7812 to bow down, prostrate oneself. *and said to his servant, Go up now, look toward the sea. And he went up, and looked, and said, there is nothing. And he said, Go again seven times.*

Elijah waited and worshipped in faith expecting results of his worship to be manifested. *And it came to pass at the seventh time, that he said, Behold, there ariseth a little cloud out of the sea, like a man's hand. And he said, Go up, say unto Ahab, prepare thy chariot, and get thee down, that the rain stop thee not.* (seven means completion.) *And it came to pass in the meanwhile, that the heaven was black with clouds and wind, and there was a great rain. And Ahab rode, and went to Jezreel. KJV.* Note that the cloud came up from the earth, as he worshipped, like a hand raised in praise.
This story illustrates the powerful effect that our worship on earth has in the heavenly realm. When we combine a congregation worshipping together, with people singing, dancing, twirling streamers, asking for the Lord to rain down on us, He will. Everyone in the midst of this spiritual downpour will be touched; you can't walk in the rain and not get wet. When the rain falls in one location everything in that location gets wet.
As we use the streamer in worship we have a two-fold purpose.
1. To welcome the Holy Spirit as He manifested in Acts.
2. To pay tribute to Him as He pours out living water upon each heart. Tribute #4530 miccah (mis-saw') A freewill offering, in the sense of flowing. *Heb./Greek concordance*

Heavenly Impact

Here is another definition for the streamer which is a wonderful description of what is seen in the spiritual realm as we use them. Streamer: A long narrow flag, banner or pennant. <u>A</u> <u>column</u> <u>of</u> <u>light</u> <u>shooting</u> <u>across</u> <u>the</u> <u>sky</u> <u>in</u> <u>the</u> <u>aurora</u> <u>borealis.</u> <u>To</u> <u>leave</u> <u>a</u> <u>continuous</u> <u>trail</u> <u>of</u> <u>light.</u> <u>To</u> <u>give</u> <u>forth</u> <u>a</u> <u>continuous</u> <u>stream</u> <u>of</u> <u>light</u> <u>rays</u> <u>or</u> <u>beams;</u> <u>shine.</u> *English Language, Fourth Edition.Copywright 2000 by Houghton Miffin Company.*

We wouldn't normally think of the streamer as a pennant, but it is long and narrow, and the word pennant has a wonderful definition; *Pennant*; The award given to the champion (syn. Crown)
Pennon, streamer, waft. A tangible symbol signifying approval or distinction. *WorldNet 2.0, Princeton University.*

Symbolic streamer movements

Streamer movements should flow gracefully from one into another. When you understand the symbolic language and can talk with your hands through the streamer it is exciting and powerful. *Ps.18:34 He teacheth my hands to war, so that a bow of steel is broken by mine arms.*
As you are changing the atmosphere you are drawing and releasing those in your midst into another spiritual dimension.

The verb for stream is streaming. Its definition fits what we are doing. Streaming: A technique for transferring data (information) in such a way that it can be processed as a steady and continuous stream, (turning data into action.) *Crystal Online Dictionary.* Data from strategic command-the throne room- into our sphere, to change our atmosphere.
A symbolic unspoken declaration of what the Lord is doing in our midst. We are symbolically declaring the Lord's will to be done on earth as it is in heaven.

The Streamer

One of the secrets of making the streamer flow gracefully is in the use of your wrist, instead of your shoulder or arm.

You can actually use the streamer in a small area if you use your wrist instead of your whole arm. Another tip for when you are getting started is to make large circles.

After practicing making the larger circles you can move to smaller circles and speed up the movement. The effectiveness isn't always in the speed; it is in the clarity of one movement flowing smoothly into the other.

The streamer will follow the tip of the rod so if you extend it to make large circles you will avoid getting tangled in it. After practicing you can move into smaller circles and more difficult movements. If the streamer wants to fold or wrap around itself, you don't have to stop and untangle it. Make several forward up and down movements in quick succession and the streamer will straighten itself out. If done correctly it will seem as if it is just a movement that belongs in the succession of movements you are doing. If the movement you are doing only requires one hand, then you will want to do something with the other hand, either raise the other hand to heaven, or co-ordinate it to move along with the streamer or let it rest on your waist. Don't let it hang limply at your side.

"Opening the heavens."

Hold the bottom of the rod part of the streamer in your dominant hand and make a large circle above your head in a clockwise, horizontal direction so the streamer is flowing in a large circle above your head.

Begin to turn in a circle in the same direction that the streamer is traveling as you do this. Extend your opposite hand straight up in the air so the streamer is twirling and your hand is raised in the center of the circle that the streamer is making.

As you turn, make a pushing outward motion with palm of that hand, away from you as if you are opening the heavens.

Heavenly Impact

As you are slowly turning in a circle (don't get dizzy) and making this movement, you are symbolically opening the heavens, creating a portal above the worship, inviting the Spirit of the Lord to come into the midst of His people.
Matt. 18:18 Truly I say unto you, Whatever you bind on the earth shall occur, being bound in heaven and whatever you loose on earth shall occur being loosed in heaven. Interlinear Bible. As we are streaming data from the throne room, we are loosing Gods purposes directly into our midst.

" Revolutionizing your atmosphere."
As you are turning with your arms up in the air, each circle you complete is called a revolution. As you move around making these circles you become a revolutionizer!

"Holy Spirit descending into our midst."
(The streamer can flow right into this movement from the opening of the heavens movement easily).
Point the tip of the rod to the heavens and make a quick zigzag, back and forth movement from the ceiling all the way down, then whoosh it up high again. Repeat this while standing straight forward or moving in a circle. Some people make small circles from the heavens down, but unless you are experienced you can quickly tangle the streamer around the rod and around yourself. If you can make this small circle movement it is very beautiful. Either of these movements symbolize the Holy Spirit descending into your immediate sphere of influence bringing with him the fire of God into our midst.

"Tongues of Fire settling on each person,"
Point the tip of the rod upward and make a waving motion up and down about at waist level or a little higher while circling. This is symbolizing tongues of fire from above, settling upon each person enabling them to witness boldly in the Holy Spirit as the new covenant believers did in acts.

The Streamer

Acts 2:3 and there appeared unto them cloven tongues like as of fire and it sat upon each of them.

"The Heavens declare the Glory of the Lord!"
Twirl the streamer in a number eight figure above your head as you turn in a circle while looking up, with your other hand raised up to the Lord. The figure eight consists of two circles the first circle is clockwise; the second is counterclockwise, flowing continuously. This movement can be done overhead, at the side or in front of your body. *Ps.19: 1 The heavens declare the glory of God; and the firmament sheweth his handywork.*

"Break up the fallow ground of hearts."
Whip the streamer up and down in an exaggerated movement forward and backward over your head-as you would use a whip. You can extend the hand that doesn't have the streamer in it, palm up and slap the rod down on it as you are swinging the streamer forward and backward. *Hos.10:12 Sow to yourselves in righteousness, reap in mercy; break up your fallow ground: for it is time to seek the LORD, till he come and rain righteousness upon you.*
Recently a woman called to share a testimony concerning this movement. She said that the pastor had the congregation walk amidst those performing this movement as a symbolic enactment their agreement with the Holy Spirit breaking up the fallow ground of their hearts. They did this in such a way as to not get hit by the streamers. The Holy Spirit manifested dramatically.

"Sowing seed for a harvest of righteousness."
This movement is a picture of an actual sewing term. It is called a running stitch. You hold the rod out in front of you and turn it in a big circle in a vertical, clockwise motion. As you are stretching out your arm in front of you making these circles symbolizing seed being sown or planted, turn your body in a clockwise circle, the same direction that you are sowing in.

86

Heavenly Impact

Symbolically you are saying the seed is being sown for a mighty harvest in every area of your life and of those in your midst or those you are interceding for who might be in other locations. *Hos.10:12 Sow for yourselves righteousness; Reap in mercy; Break up your fallow ground, for it is time to seek the Lord, till He comes and rains righteousness on you.* (This scripture says to break up and then to sow.)

"Reaping the Harvest."

Swing the streamer from side to side at about knee level-as in swinging a sickle to reap a harvest. You are symbolically harvesting, while prophetically calling forth harvesters.
Luke 10:2 therefore said he unto them, the harvest truly is great, but the laborers are few: pray ye therefore the Lord of the harvest, that he would send forth laborers into his harvest.
Rev. 14:15 And another angel came out of the temple, crying with a loud voice to him that sat on the cloud, Thrust in thy sickle, and reap: for the time is come for thee to reap; for the harvest of the earth is ripe.

"Giving praise up to the Lord."

Make circles in a vertical motion from the ground up as high as you can towards the heavens; keep repeating this movement while circling.

"Heaven and Earth"

Circling above your head symbolizes the heavenly. Circling below the waist symbolizes the earthly realm. *Ps. 69:34 Let the heaven and earth praise him, the seas, and every thing that moveth therein.* As we twirl and whirl with the streamer there is a receiving of information (streaming, enacting) coming directly from the throne room to us, as we receive the information we pass it along in a continuous fluid like motion.

"Open up the Earth"

As you circle the streamer in a horizontal position below the waist, use your other hand to make a pushing open movement in the center of the circle. Then change the direction of the circle to vertical and raise the streamer in circles up to the heavens unto the Lord symbolizing praise coming forth from the earth.

As you use the streamer the Lord will lead you to perform other symbolic movements which fit your situation or what He wants to do in your midst at that particular time.
Testimony concerning the streamer:

Recently while at a seminar in another city, I was dancing in the front of the church during the worship, at the invitation of the pastor in charge. I was adorned with a streamer we call the Sword of Grace. I was enacting, through the vehicle of dance, the movement of opening up the heavens. I was following that movement with the other movements symbolizing the Holy Spirit coming into our midst with tongues of fire settling on each person, convicting and empowering each one. I started out to the right of the aisle about five seats in. As I moved across the front of the church to the other side, continuing to do this movement of opening the heavens, suddenly a man from the back of the church jumped up and came running up the aisle to the front.
When he reached the front he made a right hand turn and went over to the exact place I had just left and fell to his knees crying. Several pastors who were there went to him. He didn't speak English so they got an interpreter who said that the man told him that when the music began to play he felt the power of God come upon him and a voice told him to run to the alter to repent for his sins, ask forgiveness and ask Jesus into his heart and life. It scared him and he did just that.
There was an intercessor who was sitting in the second row who called me to her side after the worship. She asked me what was the name of the worship instrument I was using. She shared with me that as I was enacting the open the heavens movement, which she didn't know what that was, she saw, in the spirit, the heavens open above the church. Then when the man ran up and fell down in repentance in that exact spot, the Lord confirmed the vision to her. I wasn't the only person using the streamer.

Heavenly Impact

There were others in the worship service scattered around the sanctuary using flags and other streamers and tabrets, all for the common goal of assisting the worship team and the congregation in the opening of the heavens in ministry unto the Lord.

 This happened without a word being preached. The atmosphere was changed with the worship and the presence of the Lord came down into our midst.

Another testimony:

One sunday morning as worship was about to start at our church, the county transportation bus came into the parking lot and dropped off a lady. She came into the church slowly walking with a walker. She was crippled with arthritis. She made her way in and sat down in a pew, in an aisle seat about half way up to the front. I went over to welcome her and sat down to visit with her. She said she had been a Christian since a child and had wanted to come to church because she hadn't been to church in a long time because of living in the nursing home. She told me that she had a type of crippling arthritis.

 The worship music started. After a few songs the ushers went to the front to prepare for us to take communion. As they were doing this the lady said to me rather loudly "What are they doing?"   I answered," They are preparing to pass the communion." She said,"It reminds me of the Catholic Church. If they are doing this like the Catholic Church I am going to leave right now!" She said this rather loudly so others around could hear her. I replied, "They are saying a prayer," which they were, but she couldn't hear it. She said, "Oh, then that is ok, but I don't want anything to do with anything Catholic." Communion came around. She partook.

After communion, worship continued. I stepped out into the aisle and began to worship with a streamer we call the Sword of Grace. About the third song I suddenly felt an unseen presence on either side of me. I asked the Lord what it was? The Holy Spirit said,"This is Grace and Mercy!"

The Streamer

 The song we had been singing finished and a new song started. Some of the words were: we cry mercy. I thought to myself, if I can take Grace and Mercy over to this lady and they touch her, she will be healed.
I began to move over to my right and I noticed immediately that I stepped right out of the anointing. So I stepped back, it was there again. I tried it again, and the same thing happened! I asked the Lord "What is going on? Why can't I take Grace and Mercy over to this little lady and touch her, and she be healed?"

The Holy Spirit said to me, "I can't extend Grace or Mercy because she won't extend Grace or Mercy. Her bitterness has crippled her." I thought immediately of a couple of scriptures concerning this word.
John 4:15-16."For if you forgive men their trespasses, your heavenly Father will also forgive you. But if you do not forgive men their trespasses, neither will your Father forgive your trespasses.
Matt.6:12 "And forgive us our debts, as we also have forgiven our debtors.
Heb.12:15 Looking *diligently lest any man fail of the grace of God; lest any root of bitterness springing up trouble you, and thereby many be defiled*. Trouble: The growth of a poisonous plant. *Heb./Greek concordance.*

I felt compassion for her. I wanted to help her. After the song ended a prophetic word came forth from someone in the congregation that the Lord's Mercy and Grace were present in our midst, and those who would like a special touch should come forward. The woman said she had to be going because the bus would be coming soon. I helped her outside and got her a chair to sit in while she waited for the bus. I sat with her. I wanted to give her an opportunity to extend forgiveness and to receive the grace and mercy she so desperately needed. I asked her if I could pray for her and she said, "Yes please do, because I am in a lot of pain." I told her that before we prayed I wanted to talk to her about how she had reacted to the thought that the men at the front of the church might be doing something that reminded her of the Catholic Church and how she sounded like she had bitterness towards the Catholic Church.

She spewed forth a bunch of vile things concerning that subject. At that point I decided we couldn't waste any time- in case the bus came so I spoke to her the scriptures which had come to my mind and that if she would extend forgiveness then the Lord could forgive her. I told her that I had many born again Spirit- filled Catholic friends who loved the Lord and were most certainly saved.

She exploded. I had thought she was frail! The spirit of bitterness and anger isn't frail. To make a long story short, she refused to extend grace, and wouldn't let me pray with her or for her because I had Catholic friends who I actually believed were saved. The bus came and she hauled her crippled body up the steps of the bus and went back to the nursing home with her misery. I don't intend to infer that anyone who has arthritis or another disease is in sin. Every case is different. I just want to relate what the Lord showed in this woman's case, so each person reading will realize the importance of forgiveness if they don't already.

We don't want to give the enemy any legal right to block or hinder our worship to our Most High God and the reaction in the heavenlies that happens as a result of the worship.

The important thing to remember is our goal and purpose for using the streamer. We enact the opening of the heavens over our worship, praise and intercession to prepare a welcoming atmosphere for the Holy Spirit to come into our midst in a mighty way and touch each one for His purposes, and to work in unity with the worship team to accomplish this.

Chapter 8
Mat-teh'
מטה

"The Rod of Testimony"

The word mateh or mat-teh' is the Hebrew word for rod. The double t is primarily to show that the accent is on the second syllable.
Mat-teh': branch (as extending); a rod, whether for chastening, (fig. correction), ruling, a staff, a support of life, e.g., bread: rod, staff, and tribe. *Heb. /Greek Concordance*

Translators have used three other words interchangeably throughout modern scripture to describe this mat-teh' or biblical rod. These words are stave, staff, and scepter.
The descriptive definitions of the stave and rod reveal that these two instruments were similar in appearance. The staff and the scepter have different physical descriptions.
There are 78 references to the word rod. 42 of these have this same root word (mat-teh') which points to the divine governmental rod of authority, also called "The rod of God ."

 Scriptures used in this chapter for the rod and stave reference back to the word Mat-teh'.
Ex.4:20. Then Moses took his wife and his sons and set them on a donkey, and he returned to the land of Egypt. And Moses took the rod (mat-teh') of God in his hand.

Biblical roots of the Mat-teh' as a symbol of authority.

There is a name scholar's and theologian's alike use for the Bible, this word is the Canon. The Bible or the Canon is the written laws and teachings of God. The word Canon is derived from the Greek word Kanon meaning, reed, spear, straight stick, a rule of measure, a standard, Because it is used for measuring, it adheres to a standard. Some would compare the term "God's rod of authority" the Mat-teh', that Moses used as having a like definition as this word, Kanon: God's standard for rule. Words such as, ruling, guiding, chastening, and correction are found in the definitions of both the rod and the stave.

The Mat-teh'

This tells us that the Mat-teh' is an instrument which symbolizes authority.
Rev.11:1 And there was given me a reed like unto a rod; and the angel stood, saying, Rise, and measure the temple of God, and the alter, and them that worship therein.

Stave
בד

Stave is another word for Rod.

Stave: bad, pole, branch of a tree, bar for carrying.
Maqqel: a stick with leaves on, or for walking, striking, guiding, rod, a staff. A synonym. for the Hebrew word Mat-teh' (rod). Used as staff three to four times. There are 40 references to staves.

The use of the rod or stave to perform signs and wonders points to the testimony of the Lord's presence among His people. The Ark of the Covenant, also called the Ark of the Lord's Testimony, (The presence of the Lord) was carried with two staves or rods, one on each side. *Ex.25:14; And thou shalt put the staves (rods) into the rings by the sides of the ark, that the ark may be borne with them. The staves (rods) shall be in the rings of the ark; they shall not be taken from it.*
1 Chron.15:15 And the children of the Levites bare the ark of God upon their shoulders with the staves thereon, as Moses commanded according to the word of the LORD.

Jewish tradition says the rabbis have calculated that the ark weighed close to a ton and was only symbolically borne by the Levites: the Spirit of God actually carried the weight.
We are modern day, symbolic tabernacles or arks of the testimony, carrying the Lord's presence and testimony within us. The stave or rod in our hand is as an outward symbol of the Lord's testimony being borne by us.

Physical description of a mat-teh', rod or stave.

I imagine that the ancient mat-teh' resembled the ones we use today. They were long straight poles; sometimes one end was sharpened to a point to be used as a weapon, or a tool to dig with. Modern mat-tehs' are about five to seven foot tall, about two inches around. Some are made of a tree branch with the bark either still on it or off. Some are made of large wooden dowels.

They come in all sizes of height and width and are decorated according to individual creativity. Some have been cut off the tree at a fork, with the fork on the end that is up symbolizing arms lifted in praise.

They sometimes have a bright colored cloth tied around them at the top. In the Old Testament this cloth identified which tribe the person belonged to. Some mat-tehs' have scripture burned into them, as well as the names of God. Some people write scriptures with marker pens on them. They are sometimes painted a color that is significant to the bearer of the rod.

Some may have the flags of the nations or other symbols and pictures painted or decoupaged on them. They may have fur wrapped around them, which is tied on with rawhide cords, brass keys attached, feathers, eagle decals, grapes or any other assortment of symbolic regalia attached. The possibilities of decoration are as endless as the numbers of those who use these. Every adornment on them points to something of symbolic significance to the person who uses them.

The mat-teh' was used as means of identification.

Under a decree from God each man was to have his own rod for purposes of identification.

95

The Mat-teh'

In the Old and New Testament, the Lord instructed that every man have a rod for his family bloodline or house as it was called then. The name engraved upon the mat-teh' identified who the owner of the rod was and from which tribe (house) he came from. *Num.17:2 "Speak to the children of Israel, and get from them a rod from each father's house, all their leaders according to their fathers' houses--twelve rods. Write each man's name on his rod. And you shall write Aaron's name on the rod of Levi (his great-grandfather,) for there shall be one rod for the head of each father's house.*

Jewish legend says that these twelve rods all came from the same almond tree. No one could dispute that there was any foul play when Aaron's rod budded, vs. eight.

 In biblical days the rod was an important piece of everyday equipment. It was one of the most commonly recognized symbols denoting your identity, even used as a legal means to enable you to cast a vote at the city gates, or identify yourself in a census (much like our drivers license is for us today).
We see the use of this form of identification used in relation to the first mention of the mat-teh' in the scriptures.
 Gen.38:18; Then he said, "What pledge shall I give you?" So she said, "Your signet and cord, and your staff that is in your hand." Then he gave them to her, and went in to her, and she conceived by him. Gen.38: 25 when she was brought out, she sent to her father-in-law, saying, "By the man to whom these belong, I am with child." And she said, "Please determine whose these are--the signet and cord, and staff." (rod,mat-teh') NKJV.
These items identified the man who was responsible for her pregnancy, which saved the woman from certain death. In those days a woman who was pregnant out of wedlock was considered to be a prostitute, which was punishable by stoning to death. The corresponding Hebrew number for staff in both of these scriptures is the mat-teh'.

We see the mat-teh' continuing to be used as a form of identification in the New Testament also. According to this scripture the only identification the disciples would carry would be their staff (rod).
Mark 6:8 He ordered them that they should take nothing for the journey except a staff only, not bread, not a knapsack, not a copper coin in a belt. PNT.

The mat-teh' called the "Rod of God" used to perform signs and wonders.

People who use these instruments with purpose, directed by the Lord in different arenas, could be described as a delegate or ambassador, which is one who represents a greater authority.
Ex.4:2+17; so the Lord said to him, <u>"What is that in your hand?"</u> He said," <u>a rod".</u> "And you shall take this rod in your hand, with which you shall do the signs." NKJV.

When used under the unction of the Holy Spirit the mat-teh' becomes a point of contact used to perform miraculous signs and wonders, a divine instrument used for divine purposes. It is not just a stick to brandish foolishly.

In *Ex. 7:17-20* God used the symbolic rod in the hands of Aaron, a human ambassador, to render judgment in the form of turning all the water in Egypt to blood. It became a rod of judgment over the Egyptian foreign gods and punishment to the people who worshipped them.
As Aaron performed the enactment on the earth as directed of the Lord, with the rod in his hands, he was shadowing what the Lord was doing with the rod (mat-teh') that was in His hand in the heavenly realm.

The Mat-teh'

Ex.7: 17, 19, and 20. Thus says the Lord: "By this you shall know that I am the Lord. Behold, I will strike the waters which are in the river with the rod that is in my hand, and they shall be turned to blood." Then the Lord spoke to Moses, "Say to Aaron, Take your rod and stretch out your hand over the waters of Egypt, over their streams, over their rivers, over their ponds, and over all their pools of water, that they may become blood. And there shall be blood throughout all the land of Egypt, both in buckets of wood and pitchers of stone. "And Moses and Aaron did so, just as the Lord commanded. So he lifted up the rod and struck the waters that were in the river, in the sight of Pharaoh and in the sight of his servants. And all the waters that were in the river were turned to blood. (Underlined emphasis mine).

Scripture doesn't say that they traveled all over Egypt, to hold the rod over every stream, river and pool of water. Given the difficulty of travel, time and the size of Egypt. It is reasonable to think that they might have done this enactment over one geographical area as a point of contact for all the rest of the waters in Egypt.

As Aaron lifted the rod up over the water, symbolic of the prophetic word of the Lord being lifted up, and smote the water, speaking the judgment to be rendered simultaneously over all the rivers and ponds and pools. This judgment was rendered upon Egypt by God, through the delegated authority of a human ambassador. With this scripture as a guide we see that in some cases we may use one point of contact to cover much territory. An example would be to lay our hands on a map of our city and speak scripture over it, thus covering the whole city in our prayer declaration.

This is not to say the Lord won't direct us to several or many strategic locations to complete an assignment. In this case the Lord smote all of the water in Egypt from one location. It is wise to ask Him if we can perform a strategic enactment in one location, or do we need to go to other locations in order to complete our assignment.

Heavenly Impact

The image of this demonstration is applicable today of God's judgemental authority being executed by the words of our mouth, declaring the living word of the Lord into the atmosphere in agreement with a physical symbolic action.
This scripture also reveals to us that the Lord Himself uses a rod of authority in the heavenly realm.

The Bible records many examples of ordinary people performing extraordinary acts in obedience to the word of the Lord. These are examples of people like us who were willing to be used by the Lord, for His purposes to bring about His divine will on the earth. If we are favorably inclined to this, we are prime candidates. We must not take what we are doing under the divine direction of the Lord lightly. The main purpose for the Lord to perform a sign and a wonder, with a human ambassador or through some other act of God, is for the Fear of the Lord to fall upon us and our enemies. Maybe the witnesses who are unsaved will become saved when the demons flee in terror taking with them their veil of deception that has been cast over the people. The demons panic and flee at the presence of the Lord.

The mat-teh' as a rod of testimony.

The Lord wants us to record and recount the victories that He wins for us. Writing the dates of special testimonies and scriptures on our mat-tehs' help to build our faith and exalt the Lord.
As we lift our mat-teh' towards heaven we are demonstrating a visual symbolic statement of memorial unto the Lord, which says to Him, we are remembering the times You have answered us when we have called upon You in faith believing for a miracle, and You have been faithful.

The Mat-teh'

Deborah, a judge in Israel, exhorts the people to recount (review) the miracles of the Lord towards His people.

Judges 5:11 far from the noise of the archers, (battle zone) in the places of drawing water, (peace zone) there shall they rehearse the righteous acts of the Lord, even the righteous acts towards His villagers in Israel. Then the people of the Lord went down to the gates. Amplified Bible.

They would enact previous victories, giving the Lord the glory, before they would enter into battle, or make major decisions. Sometimes the battlefront would come as close as the gates of the city. Important decisions concerning the city were made at the gates.

Ways in which the mat-teh' is used today in praise and Intercession.

We have the potential to wreak great havoc to the enemy's domain in the heavenlies when we have understanding of the symbolic significance of these rods, used under the unction and direction of the Holy Spirit.

The majority of those reading this may be mature intercessors, but for the sake of those who may be just entering into this type of intercession there are some important instructions.

It would not be wise to shake these rods in the face of the enemy threateningly, proclaiming judgments or cursing him foolishly, during times of spiritual warfare. This is exactly what he wants you to do. The more time you spend telling him what to do the less time you have to praise the Lord. The enemy is the accuser; don't mimic him, which gives him glory. You don't need to shout at him or his demons, he isn't deaf and neither are they. The word says to shout unto God with a voice of triumph. Use your energy to praise the Lord. When in doubt always look to our example, Jesus and how he dealt with the accuser. He quoted scripture.

100

Read how Michael handles a dispute with the devil.
Judges 1:9 Yet Michael the archangel, when contending with the devil he disputed about the body of Moses, durst not bring against him a railing accusation, but said, The Lord rebuke thee. Exercise wisdom.

The mat-teh' is a point of contact, which has no power in itself. The power in spiritual warfare isn't found in the enacting of a scenario with a symbolic instrument. Our strength doesn't lay in words that sound forceful or threatening.

Our source of power and authority is found in the word of God, and the revelation that comes from the Holy Spirit who tells us what to do, when to do it, (right timing) and if applicable, which instrument to have in our hand. We see that the Lord has the rod in His hand and as we praise He uses it!

Isa.30:32; And in every place where the grounded staff (rod) shall pass, which the LORD shall lay upon him, it shall be with tabrets and harps: and in battles of shaking will he fight with it. Heb. /Greek.

As we quote the word (a decree from the scripture) in the earth realm, we are laying the rod of the word of God upon the back of the enemy in the heavenlies. At the same time the Lord is shaking or brandishing tabrets, accompanied with the sound of the harp, which means to be praising, watching the enemy flee in terror. Praise the Lord! This is great! And a safe place to wage war from.

Symbolic movement with these rods

These rods are used in all types of ways. Most every movement that is done with these seems to be prophetic in nature.
They are pounded on the ground. Some have little wooden blocks that come with them which are placed on the ground to pound the Mat-teh' down on. These blocks sometimes have symbolic writing or carving on them.

The Mat-teh'

A person told me that as they were pounding the mat-teh' down on the ground they were symbolizing breaking up the fallow ground of hearts, theirs included, so they would be able to receive the gospel.

Hos.10:12 Sow for yourselves righteousness; Reap in mercy; Break up your fallow ground, for it is time to seek the Lord, till He comes and rains righteousness on you.

People might twirl or whirl with them in a type of intercession dance. This may be symbolizing many things such as the Lord coming as a whirlwind:

Prov.10:25 when the whirlwind passes by, the wicked is no more, but the righteous has an everlasting foundation.

The majority of the scripture concerning the whirlwind is speaking about the Lord coming in judgment. The Lord's will is that none would perish. His desire is for redemption.

He is the God of construction. We are called to pray a prayer of intercession, that as He comes in judgment, it will be used as an instrument of conviction, to bring the person to the full saving knowledge of the Lord and His salvation.

Some dance a type of waltz dance with their Mat-teh' as though it was the Lord. They hold the rod extended out in front of them in a vertical position holding it up and dancing around.

I have been part of a prayer team that the Lord instructed to stir water with the mat-teh' in certain locations symbolizing that He was stirring up living waters within people in those locations.

Some enact drawing a line on the ground for several different purposes. One is to circle a bloodline boundary of protection around their families or others they are praying for.

One is to draw a straight line symbolizing the enemy can come this far and no more.

Holding the rod up in the air, one is prophetically proclaiming with these mat-tehs' of historical and present day significance, that Jesus is soon to return to rule and reign over the nations with the rod of His word. *Rev.12:5 And she brought forth a man*

child, who was to rule all nations with a rod of iron: and her child was caught up unto God, and to his throne.
My husband took this prophetic scripture literally and cut our family rod (Mat-teh') from an ironwood tree. He engraved the names of God on it. There are many more significant movements that aren't listed here.
We can also stir the air symbolic as the Lord coming in the whirlwind.*Jer.30:23 Behold, the whirlwind of the Lord goeth forth with fury, a continuing whirlwind: it shall fall with pain upon the head of the wicked.*

The enemy has a rod.

Ps.125:3 For the rod of the wicked shall not rest upon the lot of the righteous; lest the righteous put forth their hands unto iniquity.
The enemy has a rod that he has been given a certain amount of authority to use on the righteous if we allow sin in our lives.
There is a voice that the enemy doesn't want to hear coming out of our mouths. It is the rod of authority in the spiritual realm, (the glorious word of God) which will turn things around as we repent before God, thus laying the rod of the enemy upon his own back.
Is.30:30-31 And the Lord shall cause His glorious voice to be heard, and shall show the lightening down of His arm, with the indignation of his anger, and with scattering, and tempest, and hailstones. For through the voice of the Lord shall the Assyrian (our present foe) be beaten down, which smote with a rod. KJV.
Have you ever said or heard someone say; " I feel like I have been beaten with a stick" Maybe a helping of introspection should be the next item on your menu if you feel this way. I have heard it said that when we knowingly sin we spiritually put a satellite dish on our head that emits a signal.
The enemy recognizes this welcome signal, He comes through this open door into our lives and makes himself at home, creating a common ground with him, making us a lawful captive, moving us out of the throneroom of grace into the courtroom of judgment.

The Mat-teh'

The accuser then has a legal right to wreck havoc in our lives. *Is.49:24-25 KJV.* refers to the lawful captive.

Jesus didn't have a common ground with the enemy and the demons knew it. He had complete authority over them and they didn't want to be anywhere that He was.
Luke 4:34 Let us alone what have you to do with us, what have we in common, Jesus of Nazereth?

The moment Jesus willingly became a curse for us and took on our sins, (creating common ground) the enemy didn't waste any time. He had a legal right in the spiritual realm, which manifested in the physical realm. Jesus received the judgment written for the crime of sin.
Isa.53:5 But He was wounded for our transgressions, He was bruised for our iniquities; the chastisement for our peace was upon Him, And by His stripes we are healed.

 From the accounts of the crucifiction the enemy uses symbolic enactments against the kingdom of God. The Soldiers mocked Jesus with symbolic enactments:

Matt. 27:27-31. Then, when the governor's soldiers took Jesus into the praetorium,[1] they gathered the whole cohort[2] around Him. And after they stripped Him they put a scarlet cloak on Him, and having woven a crown from thorns they placed it upon His head and a reed in His right hand, and falling on their knees before Him, they mocked Him saying, "Hail, King of the Jews."
Then after they spit on Him they took the reed and beat on His head. And when they had mocked Him, they stripped the cloak from Him and they dressed Him with His garments and they led Him away to be crucified. P.N.T.

Heavenly Impact

Mark 15:19 and they smote him on the head with a <u>reed,</u> and did spit upon him, and bowing their knees worshipped him. KJV.

The word reed in these two scriptures shows us several more examples of how the enemy understands and places a value upon the enacting of symbolism, and the deeper parallels they portray. When the reed was placed in the hand of Jesus it had a much deeper meaning than just a mockery of humans against Jesus. Reed # 2563 kalamos:{kal'-am-os} calamus is a quill pen, made of a plume or reed, and is a symbol of literacy and learning. In ancient days writing was once a sacred art, the calamus has traditionally symbolized individual destiny as the will of the Divine Being written in the Book of Life.
www.calamus.org

Jesus was the Living word of God. Smiting Jesus with this calamus reed was a symbolic slap in the face to Him as the Divine Living word of God. The accuser was saying among other things "You die, your word dies." Jesus paid the price. He willingly endured the beating that we should receive for our sins. By accepting our sins Jesus gave the enemy a common ground. The cost of that ground was His earthly life. If we have known common ground and we plan on moving prophetically in enactments we are asking for trouble. The enemy is well aware of any common ground he has with us. He keeps a record.

Another term for common ground with the enemy would be cursed soil. The symbolism of soil throughout the word is the heart of man.
Our first objective should always be to be sure that we are clean before God.

The Mat-teh'

Gal.3:13 says Jesus became a curse for us as He hung on the cross. If we accept His sacrifice, receiving the forgiveness it provides for us, it is our responsibility with the help of the Holy Spirit to repent for any known sin in our lives. This will turn things around, reconciling our life back to the father, in effect reversing the curse, turning the soil representing our life into fertile soil. Then the Lord will break the staff of the wicked one. *Isaiah 14:1-5 says, The Lord has broken the staff of the wicked, the scepter of the ruler.* This word Scepter is Shevet, a synonym of mat-teh'

The Hebrew children used their rods as implements prophetically.

Numbers 21:16-18 From there they went to Beer, which is the well where the Lord said to Moses, "Gather the people together, and I will give them water." Then Israel sang this song: "Spring up, O well! All of you sing to it-- The well the leaders sank, dug by the nation's nobles, by the lawgiver, with their staves." And from the wilderness they went to Mattanah.

They worshipped and praised speaking prophetically to the well, calling it forth, in faith, expecting the manifestation, due to the preceding word of the Lord, (lawgiver) to them concerning this location they were to dig in. Then they labored to see the prophetic word fulfilled! (They dug with their rods, staves.)

The scriptures make special mention that the leaders were the ones who dug the well, moving in the prophetic.
Some translations say they used their royal scepters and staves to dig the well. When leaders are obedient to the voice of the Lord the blessing flows down to the people. This show of favor given by the Lord, to the leaders built great faith in the people.

The Staff
מקל

Mak-kel-aw" or Makelot: a stick with leaves on it, for walking, striking, guiding, rod, staff. When used as a rod the leaves and branches would have been removed, if there were any. This was the type of staff that Jacob symbolically used in his breeding program. *Gen.30: 37-41.*
Shebet {shay'-bet} rod, staff, branch, offshoot, club, sceptre, tribe, a stick for punishing, fighting this is also the word for a shepherds crook. There are 43 references for staff. 17 of those references for the word staff should read stave or rod according to their root word number.

Description of the Staff

The staff is known to have a curved end called a crook.
Crook: An implement having a bent or hooked form as a shepherd's staff. *Webster's Dictionary.*
The shepherd had his staff in his hand while herding his sheep. If needed he could use the curved end to pull the sheep towards him, guide the sheep through an opening, or chastise a disobedient sheep. He would use this staff to lead the sheep to pastures and watering places.

If a sheep would get caught in a thicket by its heavy coat, the staff could be used to pull it out, or lift it out of holes or ditches, by hooking the crook under a leg. As a comfort measure shepherds would sometimes lay the staff along the back or side of the sheep as they walked together. Jesus speaks of himself as our shepherd; we are the sheep of His pasture.

Ps.95:7 For He is our God, and we are the people of His pasture, and the sheep of His hand. Today, if you will hear His voice: NKJV.

The Mat-teh'

One way to hear God's voice is to read His word. He speaks to us through his word which is the <u>rod</u> of authority for our lives.
He guides us by his <u>staff</u> which symbolizes the Holy Spirit, who comforts us, guiding us into all truth and making provision for us. *John 14:26. But the Comforter, which is the Holy Ghost, whom the Father will send in my name, he shall teach you all things, and bring all things to your remembrance, whatsoever I have said unto you.*

According to Jewish tradition the shepherd would have both a rod and a staff as their regular equipment to carry.
We saw this referenced by David in Ps. 23. David was describing a spiritual rod and staff, but it also applied in the physical realm.
Ps.23:4 Yea, though I walk through the valley of the shadow of death, I will fear no evil; for you are with me. Your rod; Your staff, and me they comfort me.
We will not be afraid during the dark times in our lives, because we have learned to trust His word which is light in the darkness and lean on the comfort and direction that the Holy Spirit provides.

The shepherds would carve testimony on their rods and staffs, maybe dates or symbols, times of supernatural intervention of God. These rods would be passed down from generation to generation. We can only imagine the faith builder a fourth or fifth generation mat-teh' and staff would have on a shepherd as they declared and proclaimed a victory in the name of the Lord while lifting this rod of authority up in the face of their enemy whether it be a beast or a being.
The story of David facing and conquering Goliath gives us an example in action of this lifting of the rod in the face of the enemy.
1st. Sam.17: 43-50 We see that David had two sticks, (staves) in his hand. One would have been the rod of testimony and

identification. He may have written testimonies on it of the times that the Lord had delivered him out of the mouth of the lion and the bear. As he lifted it up he was lifting up the testimony of the Lord. It would become a rod of God in his hand against Goliath's foreign gods. Much like the rod of God in the hands of Moses.

This rod would also be used as a weapon of offense or defense. The other was his shepherd's staff. Goliath focused on these rods. In fact he sees these as the only weapons of battle that David has. It was a fatal mistake on his part, a strategy on David's part. *Vs.43 And the Philistine said unto David, Am I a dog that thou comest to me with staves? And the Philistine cursed David by his gods. KJV.*Goliath thought he was looking at a boy brandishing a couple of sticks when in reality he was looking at a king lifting up the rod of the testimony of the King of kings.

Then David said to the Philistine," You come to me with a sword, with a spear, and with a javelin. But I come to you in the name of the Lord of hosts, the God of the armies of Israel, whom you have defied. And all this assembly shall know that the Lord does not save with sword and spear; for the battle is the Lord's, and He will give you into our Hands". NKJV. God does not save by carnal weapons. Then David ran towards his enemy.
Lifting up the rod of testimony, while declaring the word of the Lord, in the face of our enemy will move us into a new dimension of boldness and victory.
1st.sam.17:49 Then David put his hand in his bag and took out a stone; and he slung it and struck the Philistine in his forehead, so that the stone sank into his forehead, and he fell on his face to the earth. NKJV. It is interesting that Goliath fell forward (prostrate) onto his face before David, He had been running toward David when the rock hit him. He should have fallen backward in the natural. The blow of death was delivered by a stone, symbolizing the rock of the word, slung by a man. *Psa.97: 7 Let all be put to shame who serve carved images, who boast of idols. Worship Him, all you gods.*

The Mat-teh'

*Fall prostate (*face down*) before Him, all you gods.*
So David prevailed over the Philistine with a sling and a stone, and
struck the Philistine and killed him. But there was no sword in the
hand of David.

Goliath was a type and symbol of a spiritual strongman. We each
have to deal with these enemy forces in our personal lives as
David did. David trusted in the Lord to defeat him, much like we
are called to do in our lives. When we learn to sling our rock (the
word of God) at our spiritual enemies they will be defeated. We
are shooting forth lightning bolts as we quote the word. The
enemy has to stay in darkness to survive. He will flee from the
light.

The Angel of the Lord carries a staff

There are scriptures that tell us that the Angel of the Lord
Himself sometimes manifests Himself to men in the form of a
man. Be watchful!
You never know when the Lord might appear to you with a staff
in His hand. He appeared to Gideon, and Gideon didn't
recognize Him.
Judges 6:11-17 (paraphrased); The angel of the Lord came and sat
under the oak tree with a mat-teh' in His hand. Gideon said
"O sir, if the Lord is with us, why is all this befallen us?" vs. 17.
Gideon is still not convinced that he is actually talking with the
Lord. Gideon asks, " If now I have found favor in Your site, then
show me a sign that it is you who talks."

Judges 6:21 Then the Angel of the Lord put out the end of the staff
that was in His hand, and touched the meat and the unleavened
bread; and fire rose out of the rock and consumed the meat and the
unleavened bread. And the Angel of the Lord departed out of his
sight.

110

Sceptre
שֵׁבֶט

Hebrew: Sceptre: shebet {shay'-bet} rod, staff, branch, offshoot, club, sceptre, tribe, rod, staff shaft (of spear, dart) club (of shepherd's implement) truncheon, sceptre (mark of authority) clan, tribe.

Greek#4464 rhab-dos a stick or wand (as a cudgel, a cane or a baton of royalty), rod, staff, scepter, staff. There are 15 references for scepter. All of the references are in the Old Testament.

Rod in this scripture: #4464. Sceptre. A staff. Staff or baton borne by a monarch or other ruler as a symbol of authority. -The scepter, royal power or authority. *Webster Encyclopedia Dictionary* .

Protocol

The mat-tehs' speak a language of their own, exhibiting a type of unspoken authority that is spiritually felt as you are in the midst of these instruments being pounded on the floor or on a block of wood in unison. Sometimes they get a cadence going that shakes the heaven and the earth. Some believers won't be ready for this type of symbolic use of these rods. Be sensitive to your surroundings concerning the use of this instrument.

This style of praise and worship isn't for everyone, and there can be misunderstanding which could interrupt the unity of a service. Some people might be uncomfortable in the midst of those using the mat-tehs'. These percussionists should have permission before using this intercession weapon in a service.

If you are uncomfortable just move to another area where you can praise in the style you are comfortable with.

The Lord is anointing worshippers as human ambassadors much like He anointed Moses and Aaron, to use these Mat-taws' or rods in their hands, as ordained point of contact vehicles to accomplish His purposes in this earthly physical realm. For all you know they might be in dress rehearsal under the direction of the Lord!

The Mat-teh'

The exercise of symbolic enactments is another way to build our faith in the very real, very present unseen heavenly realm. Faith is the substance of things not seen. Spiritual things.

God is not finished with this mat-teh' yet. He has extended this rod of ancient days into our present age. What an honor to grasp onto it in faith raising it up in continuation with prophetic declarations that have been set forth in the word of God, thus extending it into the future.

In these symbolic instruments we see a beautiful picture. The rod and stave are representing the authority of the written word of God. The staff represents the Holy Spirit, comforter and guide. When we lean on both we will enjoy a long life full of peace and joy.

Zach 8:4-5; Thus says the Lord of Hosts; There shall yet old men and old women dwell in the streets of Jerusalem, and every man with his staff in his hand for very age. The streets of the city shall be filled with boys and girls.

Chapter 9
Billows

בל

"Birthing the purposes of God with the Billows"
113

Heavenly Impact

There is a worship and praise adornment instrument that is usually called the billows. I have also heard it called a banner, dancing silks or praise streams. For the sake of the references in the scripture and the root words for the meaning, I will use the term billows.

The definitions for the billows all express the essential nature of the billows, which is the waving up and down or side to side. We can see that almost every movement that we make with the billows can cause activation in the prophetic arena. If you want to be activated yourself and haven't been yet, this is a wonderful place to start.

There are two scripture references for billows. In each of these scriptures, the word billow has a different root word.

Included are the definitions from both the Hebrew and English dictionaries to give a broader picture. As you will see from the different meanings for the word billows, this worship adornment item is a fertile field of biblical symbolism.

Psalm 42:7 "Deep calleth unto deep at the noise of thy waterspouts: all thy waves and thy billows are gone over me."

The deep in God is calling out to the deep in us. He wants us to submerge ourselves in a new baptism (birth), yes even be overwhelmed in His divine love and purpose for our lives.

Jonah 2:3-4 "For you cast me into the deep, into the heart of the seas, and the floods surrounded me; all your waves and your billows passed over me. Then I said, I have been cast out of your presence and your sight; yet I will look again toward your holy temple". Amp. This is the cry of a repentant man.

We can't get into any situation that is too deep for the Lord. In the midst of deep areas in our lives we might feel overwhelmed as Jonah must have. God is waiting for us to turn our eyes to Him. These deep places are where we learn obedience, which is an act of worship. We are refined during the hard times. If we allow the Lord to have His way we will come out refined as gold.

The Billow

Billows #1530 (Hebrew) gal: a heap, a spring or water, <u>a wave</u> primary root; galal: to roll, to commit, to flow down, to be rolled, and to roll oneself. <u>Wave</u>: To move in waves. Moving ridge or swell of water; any movement like this; sway, to move, etc. *Webster's* . We can become the wave offering, dancing under the billows.

We could reference the symbolic movement of the heave offering to this swaying wave motion. The heave wave was characterized by the use of the shoulder and the arm, which is what is used when we raise and lower the billow.

Billows #4867 (Hebrew) mishbar: a breaker (of the sea) or wave. From # 7665 sha-bar: to burst forth, <u>to</u> <u>bring</u> <u>to</u> <u>birth</u>. #4866 mish-bare; the orifice of the womb (from which the fetus breaks forth): birth, breaking forth. When the waters break forth you know the baby is on its way. From these definitions we can see what the symbolic focus of the billows seems to have to do with water, waves and birthing.

One of the strategic movements performed with the billow is the birthing movement.

English *(Webster's dictionary)* <u>Billow</u>: A large wave, a great swell of water, any large swelling mass or surge, as of smoke, sound, etc. To surge, swell or rise like a billow. Swell: deep interior; <u>belly</u> <u>to</u> <u>swell</u> <u>out.</u>

Billows #4535 (Greek) salos: from the base of vibration.

<u>Vibration</u> #4525 (Greek) saino: to shake, to move…akin to 4579.

<u>To Move</u> #4579 (Greek) seio: to rock sideways or to and fro.

Water symbolizes deliverance among other things. Noah and his family were delivered through the deep waters, which saved the human race. Jonah was delivered through the deep waters, to come forth and birth a revival of repentance in the hearts of the people of Nineveh, which saved a town. Jonah became a sign and

a wonder which put the fear of God in the people's hearts. If the Lord uses us, it is to bring the fear of God upon the people.
Moses was supernaturally delivered through the water as a baby. He grew up to lead in the supernatural deliverance of the Hebrew children through the midst of the Red Sea, while their enemies were drowned in the same water.
Israel's enemies have threatened through the centuries and even today to push them into the sea and bury them there. (I guess they forgot to read their history.)
In the New Testament we see our deliverance through the vehicle of water, in Baptism, when we repent of our sin and symbolically bury our old sin nature under the water and rise up to walk in newness of life, we too are delivered.

Description of the Billow

The billow is a long piece of fabric made from silk or another type of lightweight fabric such as silk essence.
A standard billow is approximately 15 foot long and 45 inches wide. The length used should be determined by the size of the space that you will have to perform in. The width is determined by the type of fabric. I have seen pieces sewn together to make it wider, to produce a different effect. The longer the length of the billow the higher it billows up.
A 12 foot long billow is good to use for smaller areas and for the instruction of children. Dancing with the billows is a wonderful way for children to express themselves in worship. Billows come in many colors each being symbolic: Examples would be red for the blood of Jesus, blue for the river of God and the heavenly miraculous, red/orange for the fire of God, purple for majesty.
It is best to use a silk essence material for practice billows and use the 100% silk for the performances, for the sake of preserving the silk. The silk essence can be washed over and over if it gets dirty and will stand the test of time. It travels well also. It doesn't wrinkle too badly.

The Billow

If the billow is 100% silk and a design is painted on it, the design will show on both sides. The white silk essence will do this too, but with most other fabrics the picture will only be on one side. The pictures that are painted on billows are usually prophetic in nature, rooted in scripture, and the image possibly depicting a prophetic word yet to come to pass. It might be a picture of a memorial unto the Lord, such as a picture of Jesus with the lamb, or a cross with a dove on it.

As the billow ascends, this picture is a form of declaration that is heard loud and clear in the heavenlies. It is a sign in the heavenlies. Not only for us, but also for the heavenly host.

You can use one billow and create a beautiful message, or multiples of billows can be incorporated according to the amount of dancers and space available. To use each billow requires two people: one to hold each end.

I have seen Jean Mabry, director of the Benote Tzion Dance Company utilize volunteers (people who may have never used the billows before, including children). She will teach using two to four billows with six to eight people, and one or two extra to dance among them. She can give instruction for about one hour and present the most glorious anointed performance.

Depending on the music used, the graceful and flowing nature of the billows makes provision for those who might not think they are graceful or good enough at memorization to learn a dance containing memorization of choreography. With slower worship music, the billows can be a form of low-impact physical effort that produces high impact spiritual results.

If a person can lift their arms and walk, they can participate. The Lord uses these billows to encourage and edify a person who maybe has never taken part in this type of demonstrative worship.

The Objective of using the Billows

As we use the billows, our intent is to create a shift in the atmosphere in preparation for God's heavenly kingdom to come to earth, thus creating favorable conditions for a supernatural birthing of our symbolic movements.

 As the billow ascends and descends, it creates a vibration that causes a shaking and a quaking in the spiritual atmosphere which will cause a commotion of the airwaves changing the atmospheric condition. Demonic forces flee as we take back this sphere of authority from the prince of the air.

The King of Glory, Creator of the Universe, joins us in the celebration. Not only does the King join us, but the angelic host. Angels gather to see the word of the Lord lifted up.

Psalm 103:20 Bless the Lord, ye his angels that excel in strength, that do his commandments, hearkening unto the voice of his word.

My personal opinion is that when we use the billows with a prophetic symbolic image painted on them, which declares the word of the Lord in a visual style, there are specific angels assigned to echo this message across the heavenly realm.

The word speaks of these Heraldic messenger angels. Heraldic: heraldry, blazoning, pageantry. Herald: official messenger, one who announces significant news.

Luke 1:28 "And the angel came in unto her, and said, Hail, thou that art highly favoured, the Lord is with thee: blessed art thou among women".

Luke 2:9, 13-14 "And behold, an angel of the Lord stood by them, and the glory of the Lord flashed and shown all about them, and they were terribly frightened". Vs.13-14 "Then suddenly there appeared with the angel an army of the troops of heaven (a heavenly knighthood) praising God and saying, Glory to God in the highest, and on earth peace among men with whom He is well pleased". (Amplified Bible).

118

The Billow

<u>Symbolic</u> <u>movements</u>

Following is a step-by-step example of a prophetic enactment, utilizing the symbolism of the billow. It is a visual demonstration of the parable of the seed and the sower from the wave offering of ourselves to be used of God to produce a harvest of souls for His kingdom. Jesus says, "follow me", so we will, rehearsing visual parables. Some people won't understand what we are doing, but it is important to follow the leading of the Holy Spirit.

Matt.13:13 "That is why I tell these stories, because people see what I do, but they don't really see. They hear what I say, but they don't really hear, and they don't understand". Amplified.

Pray that the eyes of the understanding of those watching be opened. Some may do these movements with different names for them.
" The Wave offering "

Beginning with the offering of ourselves to the Lord renewing our vows to Him, committing to co-labor with the Holy Spirit, ushers in the release or birthing of the harvest of souls into the Kingdom of God. Or our symbolic birth into our destiny.
One of the definitions of the Billow has the word commit in it.
As the billows rise and fall rhythmically, and as we move about among them, we are physically becoming the wave offering.

II Cor 8:5 "And this they did, not as we hoped, but first gave their own selves to the Lord, and unto us by the will of God."

*Psalm 85:11 Truth shall spring out of the earth; (*billow ascend*)
and righteousness shall look down from heaven (*billow descend.*)
It is good to do a wave offering, one time up and down, between the movements. This gives you time to get in synchronization, especially if more than one billow is being used.
119

Heavenly Impact

This brings everyone to a stop and a fresh start - in case you make a mistake and get out of sync. with the other billows. This gives you a chance to gather your thoughts about your next movement. It helps you to all flow together. It is a beautiful, graceful way to fill the music. It can also symbolize the Lord breathing on the seed. (Breathing techniques are used in the birthing process.) This is good for those who don't remember chorography well, but want to dance before the Lord in this way. You don't have to perform as many different movements to fill the time. This is great for children.

"Commitment Kiss "

We renew our commitment to the Lord with a holy kiss movement (a kiss symbolically seals the wedding covenant.)
Psalm 61:8 "So will I sing praise unto thy name for ever, that I may daily perform my vows."KJV.
Billow ascends, which brings your arms up in the air. The people holding onto each end move together, to the center, wrists touching. As the billow is descending, they move backward bowing low returning to their position.
Psalm 85:10 "Mercy and truth are met together; righteousness and peace have kissed each other".

" Casting seed"

We want to cast seed into fertile soil. Seed thrower movement: two or more billows are crossed; when the billows go up in the air the people on either end of the <u>top</u> billow (that is the billow that lays on top of the others after they are crossed) cross over to form a tie around the others. The billows are tipped up on their sides. This will look like a pinwheel with different colored spokes. The dancers then walk in a circle.*Mark 4:3 "Hearken; Behold, there went out a sower to sow". KJV.Mark 4:14; "The sower soweth the word". KJV.Mark 4:26; "And he said, so is the kingdom of God, as if a man should cast seed into the ground."*

The Billow

" Spirit of God breathing on the seed "

Turn the spoke up now and billow up and down several times here to symbolize the Holy Spirit breathing on the seed. Uncross and billow up again. Then dancers can be dancing around under the billows with streamers, flags, tabrets, veils or anything else you use as a tool to enhance the worship. Move into line across from each other again. We can compare the seed concept to the parable of the mustard seed.

Matt. 13:31 Another parable put he forth unto them, saying, The kingdom of heaven is like to a grain of mustard seed, which a man took, and sowed in his field:

Luke 17:6 And the Lord said, If ye had faith as a grain of <u>mustard seed,</u> ye might say unto this sycamine tree, Be thou plucked up by the root, and be thou planted in the sea; and it should obey you.

Faith in the word is as a mustard seed, to birth and to nourish and watch grow. As the Spirit of the Lord breathes on the seed it is brought to maturity and is now a spiritual baby ready to be birthed; we portray the change or transition movement before the birth.

"Change or Transition movement"

As the billow goes up, the dancers on each end move forward and meet in the center. They each move to the right as they cross to switch places. As you get to your position, the billow is coming down, turn outward or to the right so the billow doesn't twist. Dancers can then billow up again continuing the flow smoothly.

"Birthing the Harvest"

Billows line up. As they billow up they form a tunnel. The billow at the back of the tunnel moves forward, (under the other billows as they are up in the air) tipped up on its side, pushing air and the dancer who is in front of it forward as it comes to the front. The next one in line also begins to follow the first through the tunnel.

Heavenly Impact

 This should be done in succession. The dancer or dancers are moving into position so that they can be just ahead of the billow that is moving forward. In effect the dancer is the point of contact, a visual demonstration of a baby being birthed in praise. This movement is powerful in the spiritual realm however it is performed.You can use one billow and one dancer or several billows with one or more dancers.

This movement symbolizes birthing and <u>deliverance,</u> new life, new way, freedom from the depths. When a baby is born in the natural it is called a <u>delivery.</u> The baby is delivered through the breaking of the waters. (breakthrough.)

"Thresher/Harvest Movement"

We begin the thresher movement co-laboring with the Lord to bring in the harvest, keeping with Jewish tradition of the wave offering.

Isa 41:15 Behold, I will make thee a new sharp threshing instrument having teeth: thou shalt thresh the mountains, and beat [them] small, and shalt make the hills as chaff.

Mark 4:29 "But when the fruit is brought forth, immediately he putteth in the sickle, because the harvest is come."

As the first billow completes its forward movement, symbolically birthing the harvest, the dancers holding it turn around to go back the way they have come. They walk quickly along the outside with the inside hand lifting the billow up and over those going through and under them. You will be holding onto the top side of the billow only so that the bottom is flowing out and over the people that are passing under, in their walk towards the front and your walk towards the back.

When you reach the back, you turn around in an inward motion. Lower the billow about chest height in front of you, low enough to see over it. Continue to hold onto the end of the billow with your hand that is on the outside. With the other hand, hold the billow along the top.

The Billow

 It will be hanging down in front of you, as you walk through to the front. You will be going under each person walking past you on the outside with the billow flowing over you. When you get to the front, turn and lift the billow with the outside hand and begin to walk to the back, repeating the threshing process over once again.

Matt.9:38 "Pray ye therefore the Lord of the harvest, that he will send forth laborers into his harvest". KJV.

The audience will be drawn into the message the billow is conveying as they watch and listen to the words of the music.

There is expectancy in the atmosphere as the movement of the billows draws us along, taking us through the various phases of a birthing process. *Psalm 85:12 "Yea, the Lord shall give that which is good; and the land shall yield her increase".*

" Hallelujah Turn"

 A wonderful finish is the Hallelujah turn. The dancers on either end of the billow will make a complete turn when the billow ascends. They will turn in the same direction to avoid twisting the billow - clockwise or counterclockwise. As you practice this you will figure out which way is best.

 Their hands will be extended above their heads, hanging on to the billow. When we hold our hands up and turn in a circle, we are releasing all concerns to the Lord, proclaiming he will turn our mourning (concerns) into dancing. He will turn the situation around. The next two movements are great conclusion movements.

"Zap Movement"

Zap: used to signify sudden, swift action or change. A zap is when you hold the billow on the ends with tension, as you raise it up quickly, it makes a snapping noise.

Heavenly Impact

The sound it makes gives me the impression of chains being snapped in the spiritual realm. It is a very effective movement to be used where you want a sound of punctuation.

"The Rapture"

There is another movement that is a very effective conclusion. It is called the rapture.
Those on either end of the billows need to billow up as high as possible then release. The billows fly up into the air and it can be a spectacular ending. If you get the right snap as you release, sometimes it makes a twirling movement almost like a tornado.
The movements I have shared are compliments of Jean Mabry, Director of Benote Tzion Dance Ministry Team. You can contact her for more information. www.garments-of-praise.com

Chapter 10
The Prayer Shawl
אהל

"A sacred tent or prayer closet"

Heavenly Impact

The Prayer Shawl is one of the most sacred and precious symbols to the Jewish faith. past and present.

It has several biblical names such as Talith, Talis, Talit or Prayer Shawl. It is also known as a canopy, shroud, cloak which envelopes the Jew physically and spiritually in prayer and celebration. We find mention of it first in Numbers.

Numbers 15:37-41 And the LORD spake unto Moses, saying, Speak unto the children of Israel, and bid them that they make them fringes in the borders of their garments throughout their generations, and that they put upon the fringe of the borders a ribband of blue: And it shall be unto you for a fringe, that ye may look upon it, and remember all the commandments of the LORD, and do them; and that ye seek not after your own heart and your own eyes, after which ye use to go a whoring: That ye may remember, and do all my commandments, and be holy unto your God. I am the LORD your God, which brought you out of the land of Egypt, to be your God: I am the LORD your God.

Deut. 22:12, Thou shalt make thee fringes upon the four quarters of thy vesture, wherewith thou coverest thyself.

These fringes on each corner are the most important feature of the prayer shawl. They are pronounced teet-zeet in modern English.

Fringes #6734 tsiytsith {tsee-tseeth'} fringe, tassel which the Israelites wore on the borders of their garments.

 Ribband of blue #6616 cord, thread twisted. *Heb./Greek Concordance.*

 Border #3670 {kaw-nawf'} corner, border and quarter. wing, extremity, edge, winged, border, corner, shirt. *Heb./Greek concordance.*

The fringes, called tsitsit in Hebrew. Kraspedon in Greek, were placed on the corners of the outer garment, which was larger than the current prayer shawl and looked like a poncho with tsitsit. This was like a sheet with a hole in the middle for the head. The front piece was tied behind the back, and then the back was lapped over and tied in front.

The Prayer Shawl

This is the seamless garment in *John 19:23-24 Then the soldiers, when they had crucified Jesus, took his garments, and made four parts, to every soldier a part; and also his coat: <u>now</u> <u>the</u> <u>coat</u> <u>was</u> <u>without</u> <u>seam,</u> <u>woven</u> <u>from</u> <u>the</u> <u>top</u> <u>throughout.</u>*
They said therefore among themselves, Let us not rend it, but cast lots for it, whose it shall be: that the scripture might be fulfilled, which saith, They parted my raiment among them, and for my vesture they did cast lots. These things therefore the soldiers did.

Recent archeological digs have found a number of these from biblical times. The most popular garment in modern times made to these specifications is the prayer shawl. There is another garment which is an undergarment like a t-shirt without sleeves or side seams (it is seamless) that is worn, usually called a Talit Katan. It has the Tzit-tzits on the corners.

We see why the woman with the issue of blood reached for the fringe in M*att. 9:20 And, behold, a woman, which was diseased with an issue of blood twelve years, came behind him, and touched the hem of his garment.*
 We find the same account by another writer.
Luke 8:43- 44 And a woman having an issue of blood twelve years, which had spent all her living upon physicians, neither
could be healed of any, came behind him, and touched the border of his garment: and immediately her issue of blood stanched.

We know this hem, border is the tsitsit because the Jewish translators who translated the Hebrew Scriptures into Greek used the Greek word kraspedon for tsitsit and kraspedon is used in the gospels where tsitsit would be appropriate.
Jesus used the prayer shawl in Mark 5:41. The raising of Jarius' daughter. We know that Jesus was wearing a Talit at that time because of the reference to it regarding the woman with the issue of blood, after Jesus and Jarius had started on the way to

Heavenly Impact

Jarius's home. At Jarius' home Jesus took the girl's hand and said "Talitha coum!" This is Hebrew for "Talit rise!" The verse goes on and says, "Translated means, maid arise" (KJV) and "My child get up." (NIV) The Greek word translated maid or child is Talitha, the Greek spelling of Talit. Coum is the Hebrew word for rise, or get up. Some Greek texts say coumi, the feminine form, which is the correct word for this verse; since Talitha is a feminine noun.

There is an Aramaic word similar to Talitha in all the manuscripts. We know that His use of the Talit in this miracle and His speaking to the Talit would have been appropriate and would have been understood by those with Him. In that case He would have placed His prayer shawl over the girl, then spoken to the prayer shawl. There is another Aramaic word that some say is the correct word for this verse. It is taly'tah, meaning lamb. This would have Jesus address her as "Lambkin", a not unreasonable assumption.
 Coumi would also be the correct verb because it is the same in Aramaic and Hebrew. My personal feeling is that Jesus would have been speaking Hebrew so I will stick with the Talit, which is the closest word to the Greek spelling. PNT. Bill Morford

Many sought to touch the tsitsit of his Talit.

Matt. 14:35-36 And when the men of that place had knowledge of him, they sent out into all that country round about, and brought unto him all that were diseased; And besought him that they might only touch the hem of his garment: and as many as touched were made perfectly whole.
Mark 6:56 And whithersoever he entered, into villages, or cities, or country, they laid the sick in the streets, and besought him that they might touch if it were but the border of his garment: and as many as touched him were made whole.

128

The Prayer Shawl

Symbolism of the numbers of twistings and knottings in the Tzee-Tzeeth.

The tassel on the prayer shawl is called in Hebrew TZEE-TZEETH. When you add the Hebrew letters in TZEE-TZEETH, you get 600. There are eight threads and five knots in each tassel.

Added together, you get 613, the exact number of Laws contained in Torah. Of the 613 Laws, 365 are negative and 248 are positive. There are 365 days in each year, 248 of which Jews are in public (not home on Sabbaths). Also, each human has 248 bones held together by exactly 365 ligaments.
The wearing of the tzit tzit is a constant reminder to Jews and others that they are servants of the Most High God of Israel. Tradition considers the tzit tzit to be a powerful shield against immoral behavior, because wearing such holy symbols reminds one to think twice about breaking Gods commandments.
Hanefesh Nat'l. Assembly of Hebrew students.http://www.hanefesh.com/edu/Tzitzit_Shawl_Prayer.htm

Every time a Jewish man puts on his prayer shawl, he is instructed to look upon the tassels which are to remind him that he is to obey all of the 613 commands of the Lord. The tassel reminds him of the great commandment, "The Lord is One," found in the Shema. The Tassel has five knots and four sets of wrappings. They numerically spell YHWH Echad (26 and 13). Therefore, the Hebrew numeric value of the tassel wrappings (between the knots) is 26 and 13 =39.

How do the wrappings spell YHWH is One? The first two are seven and eight which equals 15. Fifteen equals the numeric value of the first two Hebrew letters in YHWH – Yud and Hay. The third wrapping equals 11 the numeric value of the last two Hebrew letters in YHWH – Vav and Hay.

So, the first three sets of wrappings correspond numerically to the numeric value of the letters used to spell YHWH (Yahweh/ "Jehovah") in Hebrew.

The fourth and final wrapping equals 13. Thirteen equals the numeric value of all the Hebrew letters used in the word "one." Therefore, 26 wrappings represent YHWH and 13 wrappings represent "one." (The verb "is" doesn't appear as it is always "understood"), Jesus, Yahweh suffered 39 stripes for our healing.

Is. 53:5 But he was wounded for our transgressions, he was bruised for our iniquities: the chastisement of our peace was upon him; and with his stripes we are healed.
I Pet. 2:24 who his own self bare our sins in his own body on the tree, that we, being dead to sins, should live unto righteousness: by whose stripes ye were healed.

The Blue Thread in the tzit tzit.

*Num. 15:37 Speak to the Israelites and say to them: 'Throughout the generations to come you are to make tassels on the corners of your garments, with a blue cord on each tassel."*Each tassel was to have one longer fringe dyed the color of royal blue.

The blue was only obtained from the hypobranchial gland of a Murex marine snail that only lives in deep water in the Mediterranean. It has been calculated that it would take 10,000 snails to produce one gram of the blue dye.

The production of blue yarn and cloth dyed in the traditional way ceased many centuries ago, when the supply of snails appeared to become extinct.
Jews have never been willing to accept any other kind of blue dye, so that to this day they have no blue cord in their fringes and tassels.

The Prayer Shawl

Imagine therefore the excitement in orthodox Jewry, when, about ten years ago, it was announced that the Murex snails were not extinct after all, and it might be possible to resume production of the traditional blue dye. The Roman historian Pliny described in some detail how these dyes were manufactured in his day, and attempts to follow his method have been tried by a scientific group in the Lebanon. The flurry of excitement among those Jews anxious to be able to comply with the requirements of the Law and once again have a blue cord in their fringe and tassels may speed the efforts of those engaged in this enterprise.
 Some Jews have even gone so far as to see the revival of the heavenly blue as a sure sign of the advent of their Messiah. John V. Collyer http://www.bibletopics.com/biblestudy/14.htm

As this snail reappeared, the process to obtain the dye has been reestablished. Its use has not been widespread since the cost of a set of tzitziot cost as much as the tallit itself.
Think on this. The snail disappears at the death of Y'shua and reappears today with the rest of the signs of His imminent return.

The blue thread or Shamash, meaning servant, is wrapped around the other strands. From the Messianic point of view, the Shamash (the blue thread) points to Messiah Yeshua, the suffering servant who is also the King, as the color blue indicates. While scarlet or red is the color of shed blood, blue is the color of the bloodline; the mark of royalty. Maybe that is why it is called royal blue.
If we look back at Numbers15: 37 we see the blue thread is given to the fringe. While most English translations use the words attached, put or secured, the Hebrew word is from natan, meaning to give. The Messiah is given by the Father to fulfill the commandments. He is the only one who ever performed them perfectly. His ability to fulfill the commandments proves He has the rightful bloodline to be the eternal King. Hence, the blue thread signifies the Servant-King. The blue thread is one out of eight strands on the tsitsit.
131

The seven white strands signify the perfection, purity and holiness of God's Law.

In one sense the blue strand, Messiah, is like an eighth Law. With eight being the number of new beginnings, it shows that when Messiah was revealed He began a new Law, not destroying the seven strands representing the Torah, but beautifying them even further and adding His power to them.

The new Law was actually a Torah of ability through Him. We know this Law to be Him, the Living Torah, the Torah of Love set in our hearts by the Ruach (Spirit of God). The seven white strands are not taken away by the one blue, but rather they are completed by the blue thread wrapped with it. Without the Messiah no man can possibly keep the Law of God, but by God's power through Him all things become possible. With Him in us, as the true bloodline, our lives are purified and sanctified and we are complete. For wherever the blue thread of Messiah lives, there also lives the whole Torah bound in Him.

http://www.messianic.com/talit/chapter7.htm

If you own a prayer shawl, but it doesn't have the blue thread in the tzit-tzits, you can order four tzit-tzits with the blue thread, already tied and attach them to your present prayer shawl. You would detach the ones it has on it and replace them with the others.

The Blessing in the fringe.

When the prophet Zechariah foretold that ten men will take hold of the skirt of a Jew and say, "We will go with you," (Zech. 8:23), why should they take hold of his skirt? Why not his hands? Because the fringe of the skirt would indicate clearly that the Jew was a man of God. The Jew had a status that the ten Gentiles had not, and they knew it. The Talit with its fringes is a God ordained symbol of His holiness.

The Prayer Shawl

Such a symbol, so instructed to be holy by the LORD, has great authority when used in conjunction with faith. This prophecy is not really as strange as it seems to be at first sight, once we realize the symbolism of the fringe.
http://www.bibletopics.com/biblestudy/14.htm

The Blessing on the Crown of the Prayer Shawl

The Hebrew writing on the Atarah or crown along the top of the prayer shawl is the blessing. It says in *Hebrew "Blessed art thou, Lord our God, King of the universe, who has sanctified us with His commandments and commanded us to wrap ourselves in the tzit tzit."* The blessing is recited and then placed over the head on the outside. As the crown is placed over the head it forms its own tent.

Paul a Prayer Shawl maker?

Prayer shawl or Talith contains two Hebrew words; Tal meaning tent and ith meaning little.
Prayer Shawl making required Rabbinic training which Paul, Priscilla, and Aquila had.
Acts 18:1-3 After these things Paul departed from Athens, and came to Corinth; And found a certain Jew named Aquila, born in Pontus, lately come from Italy, with his wife Priscilla; (because that Claudius had commanded all Jews to depart from Rome:) and came unto them. And because he was of the same craft, he abode with them, and wrought: for by their occupation they were tentmakers.
The Greek word skenopoioi, translated prayer shawl makers or tent makers, is not found anywhere else in scripture or secular Greek writing. Perhaps Luke coined the word or possibly skenopoioi was used by Jewish people when speaking of making prayer shawls. Jewish men referred to the prayer shawl as a tent or prayer closet because it was placed over the head to shield the eyes while praying.

133

The Greek Lexicon by Bauer Arndt and Gringrich devotes nearly an entire column to skenopoioi. Bauer does not identify the trade, but says that it was of a technical nature and it would not have been making ordinary tents, leather working, or erecting tents, possibilities suggested by other scholars. The technical training we know all three had was rabbinic training, which was required to make another item referred to as a tent. When it was pulled over the head while praying, became a prayer closet. Making prayer shawls is an occupation that Paul could have pursued in any metropolitan area without having to haul various tools and supplies as he traveled. While Bauer leaves the trade an open question, prayer shawl making stands out as the likely single prospect. PNT.

Our Prayer Shawl becomes our Prayer Closet

Matt.6:6 But thou, when thou prayest, enter into thy closet, and when thou hast shut thy door, pray to thy Father which is in secret; and thy Father which seeth in secret shall reward thee openly. Closet #5009 secret chamber, inner room. The Greek word translated private room or closet is tameion, taken from the Hebrew word cheder, n@'aqah, referring to the talit as a prayer room or closet. With the prayer shawl (Talith) covering our heads it forms a little tent. We can shut out the world and have an intimate prayer time with the Lord. To cover is a biblical word for intimacy. This will be a private time when we can be totally focused on Him. When in our prayer closet we should pray Gods word . This is why Jewish men hold a book in their hands as they pray at the Wailing Wall. These books are available on tables set back from the Wailing Wall. Anyone is welcome to use one of them, but they are written in Hebrew! They usually pray from the Book of Psalms. Jesus was praying the Book of Psalms while suffering on the cross. Praying God's Word keeps us within God's will.

The Prayer Shawl

<u>The Lord wears a prayer shawl in the heavenlies</u>

As you place the prayer shawl on yourself with the crown in the appropriate place on your head and hold you arms out the wings of the garment are formed. With this picture in mind we can understand how the Hebrew children in covenant with the Lord could be said to be dwelling in the secret place of the Most High and under His wings. We become a shadow of what is happening in heavens. We do what we see Jesus do. We see it in the scriptures through eyes of faith. Jesus imitated the actions of His father as He saw into the heavenly realm.

Ezk.16:8 The Lord speaks to Jerusalem and likewise says, "When I passed by you again and looked upon you, indeed your time was the time of love; so <u>I spread My wing over you</u> and covered your nakedness. Yes, I swore an oath to you and entered into a covenant with you, and you became Mine," says the Lord God. NKJV. The Lord is speaking in symbolic language. The word wing is #3670 wing, extremity, edge, winged, border, corner, skirt (corner of garment) Heb./Greek.
Ps. 91:1-4. He that dwelleth in the secret place of the most High shall abide under the shadow of the Almighty. I will say of the LORD, He is my refuge and my fortress: my God; in him will I trust. Surely he shall deliver thee from the snare of the fowler, and from the noisome pestilence.

He shall cover thee with his feathers, and under <u>his wings</u> shalt thou trust: his truth shall be thy shield and buckler.

Mal.4:2 But unto you that fear my name shall the Sun of righteousness arise with healing in his <u>wings;</u> and ye shall go forth, and grow up as calves of the stall.

Heavenly Impact

Jesus will return to earth wearing a prayer shawl.

The law (Word of God, Jesus) is eternal so it stands to reason the shawl that displays the law through the symbolism of the twistings and knottings in the tzits tzits on the corners of the talit will be worn eternally. I have heard theories that when Jesus returns he will have on a prayer shawl. There are some informative word references in scripture that could validate this fact.

Rev.19:13-16 And he was clothed with vesture dipped in blood: and his name is called The Word of God. And he hath on his <u>*vesture and on his thigh a name written, King of kings, and Lord of lords.*</u>
The Greek word Himation, vesture used twice here, is the Greek word which refers to the Hebrew Talit, the same word used in *Matt.9:20-21.*
For the garment Jesus wore that the woman with the issue of blood touched and was healed, also the same word used in *Matt. 14:36.* For the garment that Jesus wore that when people touched the hem they were healed.
Rev.19:11 And I saw heaven opened, and behold a white horse; and he that sat upon him was called Faithful and True, and in righteousness he doth judge and make war. Rev.1-2 Jesus is the living testimony of the word of God.
If the prayer shawl was draped over the head and shoulders of Yeshua the tzit tzits would lay across His thigh. Which would symbolize the Word of God, the commandments of God and the name of God.

The Talit in the Tomb

<u>*Jn.20:7*</u> *And the napkin, that was about his head, not lying with the linen clothes, but wrapped together in a place by itself.*

136

The Prayer Shawl

 When Peter and John looked into the empty tomb, they saw tangible proof that Yeshua had been resurrected and risen from the dead. We read that the grave clothes were lying there but the napkin around Yeshua's head was neatly folded and in one corner of the tomb. Hebrew historians tell us that it was first of all not a napkin, but a prayer shawl. It was a sign to them that he had risen and his body had not been stolen by the Romans, due to the precise folding of it. Only a Jewish person would have known how to fold it in a certain order. The Tallit, or prayer shawl, called the napkin or fringes, in the KJV, is so sacred and personal, that Jewish men, even today, are often buried in it. All Jewish men, as Jesus and Lazarus, were buried with the Tallit about their head. *John 11:44 says - And he that was dead came forth, bound hand and foot with grave clothes: and his face was bound about with a napkin. Jesus saith unto them, Loose him, and let him go.*
Yeshua told those nearby to loose the cloth from around his head. That napkin was his Tallit. Each man has a personal and special way of folding his Tallit.

For over three years Peter and John had seen how Yeshua would fold His Tallit. Yeshua knew that when Simon Peter burst into the tomb and found it empty, Peter would think the Romans had somehow disposed of His body. When Peter saw the Tallit, as only Yeshua would fold it, he knew that the Romans did not take the body; because, if they had, no way would they have folded, or even known how Yeshua folded His tallit. One must be alive to fold that Tallit, Yeshua's way, as Peter and John knew very well. The Yeshua folded tallit, conclusively and positively announced to His disciples, He is alive! *The Resurrection The Certainty and The Proof By Jim Searchyhttp://dccsa.com/greatjoy/ResProof.htm*
 There is a protocol that the Lord has set in place for those who desire to wear a talit. Not everyone who is first interested in wearing a talit is ready to receive one. If we want to give one to someone as a gift we should not be offended if there is reluctance of someone to accept the Talit.

They may not have enough information, or it just may be it is not the time for that person.

Treat your prayer shawl with reverence. Do not lay it on the ground. Do not use it for a table covering. If you dance with it don't drop it down anywhere. Drape it around your shoulders when not using it. Don't walk on it for any reason; this would be a great offense. I know some might say I want to stand on the word of God. I would suggest you write particular scriptures on a piece of paper and stand on the paper.

You can lay on the ground before the Lord in prayerful attitude and cover yourself with the prayer shawl. The main thing is to be sensitive. Not that the Lord will strike you dead if you violate some of these unspoken rules, but why take the chance of offending Him?

Important uses of the prayer shawl in modern days.

The prayer shawl is used at all major Jewish occasions: circumcisions, barmitzvahs, weddings and burials.

It protects the scrolls of the Torah when they are moved.

The dead are wrapped in it when they are buried.

The bride and bridegroom are covered with the canopy of the prayer shawl. Some wrap the bride and groom in it, while others have the whole wedding party stand under it. I have read that three unidentified sources had the same idea for the flag of Israel. They unfurled the prayer shawl and added the Shield of David. Which is the Star of David. The 6 pointed star. The restoration of the use of the sacred Tallit is symbolic of what Jesus is doing on the earth. He is restoring our Hebraic roots and heritage through Y'shua ha Masiach (Jesus the Christ). When the Lord says in His word that these items are to be used throughout your generations. He didn't limit their use to a particular span of time.

Chapter 11
The Veil
רדיד

" Unveil my heart Lord"

Heavenly Impact

The veil has its own unique place in scripture. The are many wonderful reasons to use the veil in praise, worship and intercession, but we see that the definitions for this word point essentially to two areas.

The primary reason would be to use the veil as a tool to help create an intimate prayer closet, seeking His divine presence, coming under His covering. This would be the physical veil used for spiritual purposes.

Ex.40:3 And thou shalt put therein the ark of the testimony, and cover the ark with the vail.

We are modern day tabernacles or arks of the Lords testimony, carriers of His presence.

Hebrew word # 7289 radiyd {raw-deed'} from #7286. In the sense of spreading; a veil (as expanded): -Vail, veil. # 04598 m@`iyl {meh-eel'} from # 04603 in the sense of covering Veil: Something that conceals, separates, or screens like a curtain: a veil of secrecy.

Amos 3:7 Surely the Lord GOD will do nothing, but he revealeth his secret unto his servants the prophets.

We are symbolically covered under the wings of the veil representing the wings of the Lord. We ascend up into the shelter of the Most High. Within the veil of secrecy we receive secret revelations, treasures.

Ps.91:4 He shall cover thee with his feathers, and under his wings shalt thou trust: his truth shall be thy shield and buckler.

As you place the veil over your head and hold your arms out, the veil forms a wing effect.

Ps.17:8 Keep me as the apple of the eye; hide me under the shadow of thy wings.

Is. 40:31 But they that wait upon the LORD shall renew their strength; they shall mount up with wings as eagles; they shall run, and not be weary; and they shall walk, and not faint.

It also forms a type of tent.

Isa. 40:22 It is he that sitteth upon the circle of the earth, and the inhabitants thereof are as grasshoppers; that stretcheth out the heavens as a curtain, and spreadeth them out as a tent to dwell in:

The Veil

As we dance in a spirit of worship and humility before our king, something powerful happens. As we willingly become transparent before the Lord, we are drawn to a place of intimacy with Jesus, and He will unveil, (rend the veil) *Eph.2:14* between Him and us.

Heb.6:19 Which hope we have as an anchor of the soul, both sure and steadfast, and which entereth into that within the veil.

Another reason to dance with the veil is the opposite of coming under for intimacy. It would be to come out from under a veil of deception in any area of our lives. This is a type of deliverance acted out. This is a spiritual veil that might cover the eyes and hearts of our understanding that makes an impact in our physical realm.
The first time I danced with a veil I received some surprising revelations.

Someone had sent me a veil and asked me to dance with it and pray to see if the Holy Spirit would speak anything to me about dancing with the veil. They said the Lord had instructed them to start making veils to use in worship. This person wanted another opinion of a dancer worshipper.

 It was a beautiful veil and as I began to dance around with it in my living room worshipping the Lord, spinning and making movements which would symbolize coming under the shadow of His wings and also an unveiling movement, suddenly the Lord began to unveil my heart to me, attitudes and intents.
He showed me attitudes that I had which didn't please Him. I had a new awareness of these bad attitudes. He showed me judgments I had made, thinking they were just my harmless opinion, but to the Lord they were judgments, that placed a judgment upon myself. These things had been hidden within, veiled from my conscious thoughts, buried, deep within my soul.
Immediately I began to repent before the Lord and ask forgiveness for things that needed to be corrected in my life, as He showed them to me.

141

As I completed this time of revelation, repentance and restoration, a new wave of fresh grace and mercy began to flow over me. My personal worship time with the Lord was greatly enriched. The lady was enriched by this testimony as I hope you will be.

I love to dance with the veil and I have found it to be a strategic tool for intercession not only for myself, but also for those the Lord lays upon my heart to intercede for. If I am dancing in intercession I love to dance with a particular veil that is a light weight, hunting type of camouflage. We call it "strategic strategies" a name given to it by the Holy Spirit. As I dance with it the Lord gives me particular strategies to use in prayer. In some cases He tells me the strategies of the enemy.

2nd.sam.5:23 And when David enquired of the LORD, he said, Thou shalt not go up; fetch a compass behind them, and come upon them over against the mulberry trees.

1st. Chron.14: 15 And it shall be, when thou shalt hear a sound of going in the tops of the mulberry trees, then thou shalt go out to battle: for God is gone forth before thee to smite the host of the Philistines.

The use of the veil is a wonderful symbolic addition. It is not an essential. I don't mean to imply in any way that if you don't have a veil that you use in worship or intercession, that you won't be able to enter into a holy place of intimacy or a strategic realm of intercession. My goal is to share my testimony combined with the scripture, to exhort you to try these different methods of biblically based ideas, to enhance your praise, worship and intercession time with the Lord. Who knows what might happen!

Intercession with the veil

The message of coming out of bondage and into freedom that we enact as we use the veil can be reproduced through identification repentance on behalf of those anywhere in the world as you dance. I began to dance with this veil on top of a threshing floor prayer mat that I lay on the floor.

The Veil

It has the imprint of the world drawn on it. As I enacted this, the Holy Spirit began to quicken me to pray for this same unveiling experience to come upon my Arab sisters, that they might be set free spiritually from the veils over their physical eyes and the eyes of their spiritual understanding.

The Holy Spirit said that as we symbolically enact this removing of the veil while dancing upon the world map that we are symbolically removing many spiritual veils including the veil of deception of the spirit of Islam and other false religions that is spread over the nations. *Mal. 4:3 And ye shall tread down the wicked; for they shall be ashes under the soles of your feet in the day that I shall do this, saith the LORD of hosts.* How awesome! We are pulling down strongholds in our own lives and possibly principalities and powers over cities and nations from a safe vantage point! Hidden under His wings! He addresses them as we dance, and we just have a worshipful time! We place all of our focus on Him and what He is doing instead of concerning ourselves with the enemy.

The Lord is raising up the army of worshippers all over the world that are dancing for freedom. It is an honor and privilege to be one of the many co-laboring with the Lord as His hands and feet on the earth. We are presenting a picture of what He is doing in the heavenly realm, to release a world harvest of souls out from under the control of spirits of deception. This includes all nations.

Is.25:7 And he will destroy in this mountain the face of the covering cast over all people, and the vail that is spread over all nations.

There is another definition of the veil which reveals this other side of warfare related to it. The double-edged sword effect in the spiritual realm.
Veil: 7286 raw-dad' a prin. <u>Root;</u> to tread in pieces, (fig.) to conquer, or to (spec.) overlay:-spend, spread, subdue.

Heavenly Impact

What an awesome picture of our enemy receiving his just reward, which is defeat as we dance. We tread upon him, we subdue him, we conquer territory that he has been in control of. We are a shadow of the actions being performed in the heavenlies by the Host of the Lord and the Lord Himself!

Ps.60:12 Through God we shall do valiantly: for he shall tread down our enemies. KJV.

Ps.44:5 Through thee will we push down our enemies: through thy name will we tread them under that rise up against us.

Just as other worship items, it is wisdom to remember the veils are a double-edged sword in the spirit realm.

As we are praising and worshipping the Lord with the veil, interceding on behalf of others, and ourselves, the heavenly host is using the veil to wrap the enemy up, to tread on him, to conquer him, to subdue him under our feet.

Ps.109:20 Let my adversaries be clothed with shame and let them cover themselves with their own confusion, as with a mantle.

Ps.144:1 Blessed be the Lord my strength, which teacheth my hands to war, and my fingers to fight.

He particularly spoke of His chosen people the Israelites.

2nd.cor.3:14-15 But their minds were blinded: for until this day remaineth the same vail untaken away in the reading of the old testament; which vail is done away in Christ. But even unto this day, when Moses is read, the vail is upon their heart when their hearts shall turn to the Lord, the vail shall be taken away.

The Hebrew children at that time, were seeking after false gods. We serve a jealous God. As we dance with the veil we are spiritually unveiling the eyes and the hearts of the Jewish people, and people of all nations in preparation for the great harvest! We are the Lord's hands on the earth symbolically casting off darkness. As we intercede in repentance on behalf of sin committed against the Lord by His chosen people (stand in the gap), He will lift the veil off of the eyes of his chosen people.

144

The Veil

As you enact the removing of a veil, you can physically be turning in a circle at the same time, symbolizing hearts turning towards the Lord.

Counterfeit Veils

With a point of contact as powerful as the veils are according to scripture, we can see why they would be used by the enemy.
In ancient days false prophets and prophetesses would make kerchiefs--magical veils they called them, which they put over the heads of those consulting them, as if to fit them for receiving a response, that they might be rapt in spiritual trance above the world. *Jamieson, Fausett & Brown-Blue letter bible.com*
The Lord addresses this in *Ezek.13: 21 Your kerchiefs (veils) also will I tear, and deliver my people out of your hand, and they shall be no more in your hand to be hunted; and ye shall know that I am the LORD.*
Is.61:1 The Spirit of the Lord GOD is upon me; because the LORD hath anointed me to preach good tidings unto the meek; he hath sent me to bind up the brokenhearted, to proclaim liberty to the captives, and the opening of the prison to them that are bound;
Prison: #6495 matches the Hebrew p@qach-qowach opening (of eyes), wide (spiritual blindness.)

One day as I was dancing with a veil and I asked the Lord what would He consider my personal veil to be. I was thinking maybe he would lead me to a specific color or fabric. The Holy Spirit said your veil is a fish net.
Matt. 13:47 Again, the kingdom of heaven is like unto a net, that was cast into the sea, and gathered of every kind:
Be sensitive and ask the Holy Spirit if there is a particular veil that would prophetically speak of your ministry. My heart beat is evangelism. Of course we aren't restricted on which veil to dance with at any time. Our God is about change and transformation and we each have many giftings and callings.

Heavenly Impact

Veils can be made out of almost any material although usually
they are made of lightweight see-through polyester. Size varies
usually 45 inches top to bottom by 72 inches side to side. Some
make them like a mantle with heavy fabric. They can be trimmed
in all sorts of creative ways. Frings, tassels, beads, bells, and
imitaion stones. I have seen so many different styles and sizes.
They are personal to the person using them. Usually the colors
are symbolic so I will add a few below. Some have scripture and
a few might not.

Color symbolism

 I have read many different studies concerning the symbolism of a
wide spectrum of colors. I have come to the conclusion that each
color can have about 100 different meanings according to who
you talk to and what that color may mean to them.
Below is a short list. I have tried to show how they might
individually relate to scripture. I picked what seemed to me the
best scripture to represent each one.

Amber: Brownish-yellow Ezek. *1:4 Used* with red and copper to
represent the fire of God.
*And I looked, and, behold, a whirlwind came out of the north, a
great cloud, and a fire enfolding itself, and a brightness was about
it, and out of the midst thereof as the colour of amber, out of the
midst of the fire.*
 Bronze and Brass often used as colors representing testing. Fires
of testing *Lev 26:19 And I will break the pride of your power; and I
will make your heaven as iron, and your earth as brass:*

 As praying Christians this can translate from judgment into
conviction, due to grace and mercy. When we think the heavens
are brass over us we have the opportunity to repent, and ask for
forgiveness, quickly. The Lord is required by His law to judge us.

145

The Veil

We would wear this veil to symbolize breakthrough, after repentance as we whirl and twirl lifting it off of us, holding it up to the Lord. *Deut. 28:23And thy heaven that is over thy head shall be brass, and the earth that is under thee shall be iron.*

Brown: Earth *Gen. 1:10 And God called the dry land Earth; and the gathering together of the waters called he Seas: and God saw that it was good.* Usually symbolizes humility.

Burgundy: wine color New wine: a memorial to the cup of the new covenant, blessings, rejoicing, blood of Jesus, Bride of Christ, surrender, the fellowship of Christ's suffering.

1 Corinthians 11:25 After the same manner also he took the cup, when he had supped, saying, this cup is the New Testament in my blood: this do ye, as oft as ye drink it, in remembrance of me.

Camouflage: New life-green. Humility-brown.

The Lord will unveil His strategies to you for victory! He will also reveal the strategies of the enemy to you, to make something hidden revealed, that which had been secret and obscure as in drawing back a veil. To bring to light the mysteries of the kingdom.

Copper: Glory a mix of red and gold make copper, which we normally think of as a fire color. *Ex.24: 17 And the sight of the glory of the LORD was like devouring fire on the top of the mount in the eyes of the children of Israel.* Some use gold as Glory. I like to think of copper and gold as the Zeal of God, relating it to fire.

Cream: Prosperity. Several times in the scriptures the Lord relates the prosperity of His people symbolically to the words "milk and honey." Cream comes to the top in milk. It is very rich and fat. Mix the milk and the honey it will be cream colored. In *Gen. 41:26* The bible refers to 7 prosperous years, relating them to plump cows.

Ex. 3:8 And I am come down to deliver them out of the hand of the Egyptians, and to bring them up out of that land unto a good land and a large, unto a land flowing with milk and honey; unto the place of the Canaanites, and the Hittites, and the Amorites, and the Perizzites, and the Hivites, and the Jebusites.

Heavenly Impact

Gold: **Glory of God. The Divine presence of the Lord.** *Rev. 1:12-13 And I turned to see the voice that spake with me. And being turned, I saw seven golden candlesticks; And in the midst of the seven candlesticks one like unto the Son of man, clothed with a garment down to the foot, and girt about the paps with a golden girdle.*

A vessel full of prayers being answered. *Rev. 5:8 And when he had taken the book, the four beasts and four [and] twenty elders fell down before the Lamb, having every one of them harps, and golden vials full of odours, which are the prayers of saints.* **Favor of the Lord:** *Ester 5:2 And it was so, when the king saw Esther the queen standing in the court, [that] she obtained favour in his sight: and the king held out to Esther the golden sceptre that [was] in his hand. So Esther drew near, and touched the top of the sceptre.*

There was a glow associated with the Shekinah Glory in the Tabernacle and the Golden Lampstand. *Heb. 1:3 Who being the brightness of [his] glory, and the express image of his person, and upholding all things by the word of his power, when he had by himself purged our sins, sat down on the right hand of the Majesty on high;*

Green. **Usually associated with new life and new growth.**
Ps.23:1 He maketh me to lie down in green pastures: he leadeth me beside the still waters. **The words green pastures give us the picture of lush rich fruitfulness, It would be reasonable to assume that green could also represent the word life.**

To have a vibrant fulfilling life you need to stay fresh with new life and new growth. The word teachable ness could apply here. If you aren't teachable then there will be no new life. As you use this color you release teachable ness or new life into those in your midst.

Iridescent: **A beautifully transparent shining light that reflects the glory of the Lord within. We must be transparent before our King, and His presence within us will shine forth.**
Rev 21:11+19. Having the glory of God: and her light was like unto a stone most precious, even like a jasper stone, clear as crystal.

The Veil

And the foundations of the wall of the city were garnished with all manner of precious stones. The first foundation was jasper; the second, sapphire; the third, a chalcedony; the fourth, an emerald. Rev.21: 23-24And the city had no need of the sun, neither of the moon, to shine in it: for the glory of God did lighten it, and the Lamb is the light thereof. And the nations of them, which are saved, shall walk in the light of it: and the kings of the earth do bring their glory and honour into it.

<u>Pink:</u> Reconciliation. Pink is a mixture of white and red. When a wound is in the process of healing, the skin will be pink if it is healthy. It symbolizes the blood of Jesus, mixed with white, which symbolizes the purity of the believer as they cleanse themselves in prayer through repentance and forgiveness.

<u>Purple:</u> Used in several features of the tabernacle *(Exodus 26:1, 27:16)* and the temple *(II Chronicles 2:14);* the color of royal robes *(Judges 8:26);* the garments of the wealthy *(Proverbs 31:22; Luke 16:19* the robe placed on Jesus *(Mark 15:17, 20)*. This color symbolizes kingship and royalty. *Dictionary of Biblical Imagery.* I think of ripe grapes which symbolize fruitfulness.

<u>Red</u> or <u>scarlet</u> *Isa.1:18 Come now, and let us reason together, saith the LORD: though your sins be as scarlet, they shall be as white as snow; though they be red like crimson, they shall be as wool.* Often refers to blood atonement and sacrifice.

Red is used as a memorial to Jesus. For His sacrifice on the cross for our sins. He paid the price so we might live.

<u>Red/Gold</u> <u>mix:</u> Fire and the Holy Spirit *Acts 2 3-4 And there appeared unto them cloven tongues like as of fire, and it sat upon each of them. And they were all filled with the Holy Ghost, and began to speak with other tongues, as the Spirit gave them utterance.*

<u>Royal</u> <u>Blue:</u> Royal Priesthood *Ex.39: 1 And of the blue, and purple, and scarlet, they made cloths of service, to do service in the holy [place], and made the holy garments for Aaron; as the LORD commanded Moses.*

Heavenly Impact

Numbers 15:38 Speak unto the children of Israel, and bid them that they make them fringes in the borders of their garments throughout their generations, and that they put upon the fringe of the borders a ribband of blue:
Open Heavens. Because people generally equate the heavens as being blue. This color is used a lot to symbolize open heavens. A color symbolizing the Miraculous: Jesus was a Rabbi so He wore a prayer shawl and it would have had the ribband of blue in the corner tassels that everyone wanted to grab onto to so they might be healed. *Num.15:38 Speak unto the children of Israel, and bid them that they make them fringes in the borders of their garments throughout their generations, and that they put upon the fringe of the borders a ribband of blue.* This was the corner of the garment the woman with the issue of blood grabbed onto and was healed. *Luke 8:43-44 And a woman having an issue of blood twelve years, which had spent all her living upon physicians, neither could be healed of any,; Came behind him, and touched the border of his garment: and immediately her issue of blood stanched.*
I have a praise and worship dance overlay that is different colors of blue. My six year old granddaughter calls it my "walking on the water dress", When I wear it the garment is a visible symbolic message that charges the atmosphere, inviting the Lord to come into our midst with miracles, signs and wonders. It becomes a testimony of what I expect to see happen.
<u>White:</u> Holiness, purity. White is the color of fine linen, which reflects the holiness of the Lord. To be worn by the saints when they wed Christ to reign together for eternity.
The robes of the righteous.
<u>Yellow:</u> Perfect Love: The brightness of the sun (Son). *Mal.4:2 But unto you that fear my name shall the Sun of righteousness arise with healing in his wings; and ye shall go forth, and grow up as calves of the stall.*
<u>Silver:</u> Redemption. *Mal.3:3 And he shall sit as a refiner and purifier of silver: and he shall purify the sons of Levi, and purge them as gold and silver, that they may offer unto the LORD an offering in righteousness.*

Prophetic movements

" Laying your burdens down."

A hand on each end of the veil holding the veil up above the head with it hanging down behind you, flip the veil over in front of you as it travels through the air to rest on the ground in front of you. Next, reverse this movement. As you are throwing your hands up in surrender unto the Lord, (You have surrendered those things which tie you to the cares of this world), You have erected a throne (alter) of worship for the Lord to sit upon over your life. The double-edged sword to this movement: in the spiritual realm you are pulling down strongholds, overthrowing thrones of iniquity, sin.
As we surrender, the Lord will perform this for us, we are acting out what He is doing in the heavenly realm. *(Dan.7:9)*

"Birthing"

Birth the purpose of God for your life. Lift the veil off (a hand on each end) while stepping forward to symbolize the birthing of the purposes of God. This can be personal, regional, national or international. Entire families, cities, countries are experiencing conversion. God is desiring to create an opening to bring forth life. Just as the birth canal is enlarged for the baby to come forth in natural birth, we move through this time of transition, moving from one place to another. We will symbolically hold our arms wide and step forward, turn around symbolizing that the Lord is turning things around, making an opening for the new spiritual birth.

"Wrapped in His presence"

Wrap the veil around you to embrace the love of the father and the changes that He will work in your life for your good.

150

Heavenly Impact

The word surround is a good description for this movement.
Extend both arms out from your body. As you turn in a circle
close first one arm in and then the other for the embrace. Or both
at once. You can turn while doing this movement. I usually start
this movement with folding my left arm in and turn in a circle
with the right hand out when I complete the full circle, I pull in
that arm and take a step extending the other arm out and turn in
the other direction. Kind of like swoop the air and pulling it in
one way then another. This makes an encompassing type
movement which includes those in your midst. (like the Lord is
embracing everyone, not just you.)

" Removing the veil"

Both hands extended up in the air above your head. Each hand
has a corner of the veil in it. You swing both hands in a circle
above the head. (One hand follows the other.) You can turn while
doing this. As you complete the movement you drop the veil
down, still holding both corners, bring both hands together to
meet right in front of you and lift them to the Lord as an offering.
Then you can bring them down and swoop up and do the unveil
again.

"Worship and honor"

Put the veil over your head and extend arms so the veil forms
wings over your arms. You can do many movements with this.
You can turn with the arms out; you can raise your arms to the
Lord. You can go down on your knees with arms extended and
head bowed. Sometimes I have brought both arms to the front
and lifted them up in a sign of surrender then lower them both at
the same time while bowing. This also works for the songs that
have the words "wings" in them.

151

The Veil

"Striking the waters"

Fold the veil in two then grasp it in the middle and make an exaggerated circle swinging movement.

Ex.12:7 And they shall take of the blood, and strike it on the two side posts and on the upper doorpost of the houses, wherein they shall eat it. (The angel of death passed over these houses that they put the blood on the doorposts.)

Ex.12:23 For the LORD will pass through to smite the Egyptians; and when he seeth the blood upon the lintel, and on the two side posts, the LORD will pass over the door, and will not suffer the destroyer to come in unto your houses to smite you.

2nd.king 2:8 And Elijah took his mantle, and wrapped [it] together, and smote the waters, and they were divided hither and thither, so that they two went over on dry ground.

2.king 2:14 And he took the mantle of Elijah that fell from him, and smote the waters, and said, Where is the LORD God of Elijah? and when he also had smitten the waters, they parted hither and thither: and Elisha went over.

"Open Heavens"

Grasp a corner of the veil with each hand. Extend your hands above your head. Turn in a circle and let the veil flow out. Above your head would signify the heavenly realm. After a couple of full turns let go of one of the corners. The veil will stream out and will symbolize the opening and the release.

To do this symbolizing the release of the veil over the face of the earth you can do this at waist level.

These are just a few movements you can do. I am sure the Lord will give you many more and you can interchange movements that you can do with the other instruments to increase your symbolic vocabulary. If you want to share any movements with me to put in the next printing of this book contact me.

Chapter 12
Protocol

Because it has already been established that the Lord wants us to use these items throughout the previous chapters, this chapter will be devoted to what could seem negative problems concerning the use of the items, but they need to be addressed. Be considerate.

It is important to think of others when using these worship tools. First and foremost is to get permission from the pastor or designated leader of the location where you are planning to use these tools. Of course there will be times when you don't have to ask permission because of the location, like a worship and praise conference. Over the last ten years I have received a few calls from people who say that when they used their worship tools in their church, that someone from the congregation complained to the pastor that they were a distraction, so the pastor asked the person to please not use the item in the church.

I always suggest that if the person has bought something from Glorious Creations that they take the scriptural information that comes with every item, to their pastor and get permission before using them. This gives him the information that he needs to be able to make an informed decision about the protocol for the use of the items in the church. This protocol includes the areas that are designated for the use of these items.

In our church the pastor decided not to allow anyone in the center aisle in case someone wanted to walk up to the alter area. We can use the side aisles and across the back in our church. This works fine for us. Usually one or two at the most can be up at the front. This has a lot to do with space available.

The next hurdle comes if the pastor says he doesn't want them to be used in the church. I always tell the person that the Lord will use this situation to show them where their own heart is. This isn't about performance or attention, and we don't need to defend God or the use of these instruments. I would never counsel someone to leave their church if they didn't get their way concerning this issue.

Heavenly Impact

The Lord is well able to change minds if that is His plan. (The pastors or yours!) This is a time to trust the Lord. If you can't use your worship tool in the sanctuary during praise and worship maybe you can use it before church to prepare the atmosphere before anyone gets there or maybe you can use it in a room in the church somewhere where the intercessors meet. In some cases, after the pastor has received the information and had time to study it, he has decided to spend some time teaching on this subject, preparing his congregation to embrace this particular flow of the Holy Spirit. You always have the freedom to use the item in your home and since it is to worship the Lord with, I always find that this time at home worshipping is more precious to me, than the time I use the tools in the congregational setting.

Those in charge have to look at the big picture of what this opens up that could cause future problems or possible offenses within his congregation. One area to look at is the children who will want to use these items. Adults should take turns being in charge of an area where the children can worship. We taught classes in our church so the children would have an understanding of the importance of respecting these symbolic instruments.
Some have asked is it ok for the children to use the tools if they are considered offensive weapons in the spiritual realm. After seeking the Lord about this question and getting many different opinions from leaders, the conclusion is that the children are covered when performing with these items through their parents or church leadership. The children do need to be taught to use them and respect them. If the child refuses to obey the rules then the privilege of using the tool is taken away for that week.
If you are allowed to use the items be sensitive of the space you have around you.

Protocol

If others have to share the space be considerate, not to hit them by mistake when you are twirling or praising with any of these items. You can be expressive, but uncontrolled boldness can infringe on the rights of others. I have had some pastors ask what to do if someone in their congregation begins to use the items and this person has worldly issues they are still dealing with such as alcoholism or smoking or other problems that they may not have been set free from yet. They wondered if something would be released into the atmosphere when the person begins to wave these items etc. After prayer and discussion with others the consensus is that the Lord would be pleased if the person was to wave a banner for Him. The enemy wouldn't. Who knows the Lord might use that banner as a point of contact to set the person free as He did with the handkerchiefs of Paul!

Acts 19:11-12 And God wrought special miracles by the hands of Paul: So that from his body were brought unto the sick handkerchiefs or aprons, and the diseases departed from them, and the evil spirits went out of them. KJV.

As for releasing into the atmosphere negative things, the symbolic message the item portrays would take precedence over anything the enemy would attempt. Most banners or any other item used in this type of setting speaks symbolically of victory, healing, purity etc.

These are prophetic words that the person is declaring into the atmosphere as he uses these items. He might just get a supernatural deliverance as he dances with them.

It is good to have a place in the church where these items are hung up or stored safely. We have a coat rack at the back of our church that has been readjusted to hold the worship items that belong to the church neatly, when not being used. This is a largely unchartered territory for most of the modern day church that is being explored. Just like the early church pioneers of revival, we press forward expecting the Lord to guide us as we move by His Spirit. That is what He asks of us, be willing to stretch out our tent pegs, He will give us new territories.

155

Heavenly Impact

According to the scriptures we have reviewed in this book, as we exercise our faith, using these items He will be well pleased with us. He may even use us as a human ambassador to bring a change in our nation through our obedient enactments. He has done it many times before and wants to do it again.

I want to conclude with a few scriptures concerning this subject so that we finish with the proper perspective!

2.chron.17:10 And the fear of the LORD fell upon all the kingdoms of the lands that were round about Judah, so that they made no war against Jehoshaphat.

If the Lord uses you to perform an extra-ordinary supernatural enactment which draws the attention of men then you have been given a platform by the Lord to bring men into the kingdom. That should be our whole focus.

Th bible is consistant in this truth. Whenever the Lord moved in supernatural ways whether it be through a human ambassador or an act of nature. It was always for the specific purpose of bringing the fear of the Lord upon the people.
His reason was for people to repent and believe in Him. He doesn't want any to perish.

About the Author.

I was raised with a strong belief in Jesus, but didn't have a personal relationship with Him until I was 25 when I received the Baptism of the Holy Spirit in 1976. My husband and myself were a young married couple with a six-month old son.

We were members of a church in Naples, Florida. After several years our pastor began to teach us about our responsibility as Christians to support Israel. He invited a guest speaker named Derek Prince to come teach us. He gave us ideas of how we could best utilize our resources to help Israel and to show our love in a practical way to the Jewish people in our own community. Not to evangelize them, but to extend our thankfulness and love to them for the Jewish heritage which had given us our Bible and our salvation.

We wanted to demonstrate our support in a pro-active way for the land of Israel. We did what seemed like a simple thing to us at that time. We gave money to a ministry that planted trees in Israel. Some of our members actually went and visited Israel and lived on a Kibbutz (farm) and volunteered to plant these trees and work in the fields.
On the community level the pastor decided we would invite the local Jewish congregation to what we would call "Israeli night." We would cook and serve them their traditional ethnic dishes. Our worship team would learn some traditional Jewish songs and some Israeli folk dance songs and we could praise the Lord together.

Heavenly Impact

During the planning stage for the "Israeli night", our pastor had a heart attack. While in cardiac rehab three times a week, he met a man who was the Rabbi of the local Jewish congregation. As they developed a friendship our pastor asked him if he would be in agreement with what we would like to do. The Rabbi was enthusiastic about the idea.

The date for the night of this celebration happened to fall during the Jewish holiday of Hanukah. The Rabbi agreed to teach us about this holiday.

There was a young woman in our fellowship, Martha who had been a dance instructor before becoming a Christian. She asked the pastor if she could inquire if there was anyone from the Jewish Temple who could teach her some Israeli folk dance and we would have a team of people dance as the music played. He loved the idea. There was an older lady who was able to teach the dance to Martha. She then taught about 15 of us to dance. The great thing about Israeli folk dance is that men who might want to be part of the dance ministry, but aren't into ballet enjoy this type of dance; age doesn't stand in the way. If a person can learn the steps, they can participate.

The big night finally came. We broke bread together over the traditional meal which was wonderful. Then we went into the sanctuary to worship and praise the Lord. Jews and Gentiles together. The Lord's presence was so heavy and precious.

They were so touched to think that we would show them such love. There wasn't a dry eye in the place, them or us.

The Rabbi taught on Hanukah and all the children gathered around him at the front. He gave them each a piece of chocolate as he shared the wonderful miraculous story about the Festival of Lights, (Hanukah.) The children sat spellbound as we did, while he taught.

On Monday morning the pastor's phone began to ring. It was Rabbis' from other Temples in our area inviting us to come visit them. They would cook a meal for us and we would bring the worship team and the dancers'. We would have a wonderful time of fellowship together.

About the author

They said that we were an inspiration to them.

To us it didn't appear that they had many young people in the different congregations that we visited at that time. The worship brought such life and spiritual excitement about their Jewish roots. It became a bridge which connected them at a deep inner level to their past Hebrew heritage.

We began to travel about once a month to a different Jewish Temple. The dance ministry was called Psalm Dance. We met once a week and learned more dance movement vocabulary for different styles of worship dance. We were invited to many churches, nursing homes an unwed mother's home and other places to minister through the vehicle of praise and worship dance.

A year later when it came time for our second Israeli night we really didn't have enough room in our church. More than the one congregation wanted to be involved. Beginning with the third year the Pastor and the Rabbi decided to turn it into a big once a year Israel benefit celebration, open to all.

We rented a large Ballroom at the Ritz Carlton Hotel and invited anyone who wanted to come. We drew a large crowd of Christians and Jews, who wanted to have a night of listening to the songs which had such a rich and vibrant heritage and to watch the dance and dramas presented. Many said they could close their eyes and imagine themselves in Israel. Quite a few said that the Israeli nights activated within them the desire to go and visit Israel. A lot of money was raised through this celebration of Israel for the Hadassah Children's Hospital in Jerusalem. This went on for about 10 years, until both the pastor and the Rabbi retired. The new leaderships directed ministry into other areas. In retrospect we can see how the Lord wanted us of us involved in this love for Israel into all areas of the country to be able to influence many through the teaching we had received.

I am sharing this testimony in detail because I believe and hope there will be those reading this who will be activated to support Israel in some way, or just show a kindness to the people of the Jewish community where you live. You will bless the Lord.

Heavenly Impact

Zechariah 2:8 For thus saith the LORD of hosts; after the glory hath he sent me unto the nations which spoiled you: for he that toucheth you toucheth the apple of his eye.

Time flew by and before we knew it 20 years had passed, most of them active in the dance ministry.
 It was time for that season to come to a close. The pastor and the Rabbi retired the same year. The new Pastor had a different focus and the new Rabbi did too.
At the time this was very hard for those of us who had been so involved in the dance ministry for so many years. The Lord had His plans. One by one we all began to be called to move to other states. As for my husband, myself and two of our children, we came to Michigan in 1996. Our oldest son and family still live in Florida.
We settled in an Assembly Of God Church in Coldwater.

The Pastor was interested in our past church life and as we shared what we had done in Florida concerning the dance portion, he asked if I would be willing to dance at special times and maybe teach the children and women some dances. I said yes, and that has continued to this day. We do have a dance ministry called Shekinah, which means God's Glory.
We don't meet regularly as a dance team, but whenever the pastor asks us to, we put together a dance and minister.
We use the symbolic instruments in our church regularly and I dance every Sunday that I am there. I pray that the Lord will send us an anointed worship dance leader that can teach those who want to be a part of dance ministry weekly class. I don't proclaim to be a dance teacher. I know my focus is to teach dancers and others on the symbolic instruments of adornment.

160

About the author

I had used many of the worship adornments, which I have written about in "Heavenly Impact" in dance without giving a thought to their biblical roots. While using these items we could see that in addition to worship and prayer they affected both the people watching and the atmosphere in the place we were worshipping. We didn't understand the significance of these items until I began to biblically research each one. After researching, they changed from being just a pretty adornment used with the dance, to a tool or weapon we could use symbolically to visually demonstrate what the Lord was doing in our midst.

 Example: Opening the heavens for the Holy Spirit to come into our midst, settling on each person to break up the fallow ground of our hearts in preparation of receiving the seed that will be sown, to reap a harvest. (See streamer chapter).

It is clear to me the spiritual and physical sowing that we did into Israel all those years prepared us to birth the ministry we call Glorious Creations, which we established in 1997. Some of us women formed a team and began to travel and teach on these items. We made them and sold them at conferences. We created a website. We developed a network of distribution across the United States, exchanging with other ministries, selling each other's items for the common promotion of the Kingdom of God and the symbolic adorning of the bride in anticipation of the return of Jesus.

Our team travels extensively nationally and internationally conducting Heavenly Impact Seminars. We teach/demonstrate and activate Gods word into the atmosphere through the vehicle of worship, praise, dance and adornment with these symbolic instruments. As people are in the midst of this they can be saved, delivered, filled with the Holy Spirit or touched in many other ways, as the Lord chooses to move upon them. The different prophetic movements, which are explained in each chapter, speak the soundless language, which people hear and respond to at a deep inner level.

Heavenly Impact

This is all about Worship and praise on earth as it is in heaven. This is eternal.

The Lord spoke to my heart about writing this book about one year before Aimee Kovacs prophesied over me that I would write a book on praise, worship and intercession. I just didn't have a clue how to go about this. Her prophetic word moved me to action.

I don't want this to sound like it was an easy thing to do, just sit down and write a book. At times it felt overwhelming and that I wasn't making headway, but I would always go back and read the prophetic word and scriptures and continue on.

I am so thankful for my wonderful husband, family and dear friends past and present who have encouraged me to keep on keeping on. I exhort each of you to examine the prophetic words that have been spoken over you and pray that you might be able to put them into action if you haven't. The Lord is faithful to His word; if you have a prophetic word you have been praying over He will bring it to pass if you co-labor with Him. That means you start.

He gave me two scriptures about the same time he told me to write the book and I have kept them and prayed over them often. Now I write them as a memorial to the Lord for His faithfulness.

Hab. 2:3 For the vision is yet for an appointed time, but at the end it shall speak, and not lie: though it tarry, wait for it; because it will surely come, it will not tarry.

Ps. 68:11 The Lord gave the word: great was the company of those that published it.

Jeanette Strauss

I close with this blessing for each and every one.
Numbers 6:24-26 The Lord bless thee, and keep thee: The Lord make His face shine upon thee, and be gracious unto thee: The Lord lift up His countenance upon thee, and give thee peace.

Heavenly Impact -The cover

Original Oil painting, 24x36. Painted by *Leslie Young Marks.* "Painter of Truth." The cover of *Heavenly Impact* depicts Jesus, The Christ, the son of the living God seated on the Throne. He personifies the mercy seat that is covered by the wings of the Cherubim atop the Ark of the Covenant. A visible symbol of God's presence.

A rainbow encircles the throne. Beginning with emerald green, the color that John the beloved saw in *Rev. 4:3.* The colors continue to unfold revealing the full spectrum that creates a perfect covenant rainbow. The top portion is God's covenant with us. The reflected color in the earth realm denotes the completion of the covenant as we respond to His grace. We are yoked together with Him and the fulfillment of His promise of restoration.

One color transitions into another flooding the earth with the beauty of the Lord. The many facets of His divine nature and the diversity of His creation. As the colors converge they display the harmony that will be realized as the body of Christ is joined together in love. As we become one with each other and one with Him, we will truly shine forth His Glory in the earth.
The King of kings is extending His scepter, bidding His bride to boldly approach the Throne of Grace. He is imparting His favor and granting her request as she delights herself in Him and becomes His pleasure.

 The act of worship in spirit and in truth releases the power of heaven represented in the elements of nature. The wind, the whirlwind, fire, sun rays, rain, waterfall, river of Living water and vapors of smoke all symbolize the interaction of an omnipotent God with His creation in response to worship and intercession.

Heavenly Impact

We are in a season when signs, wonders and miracles are being released at a new level. Worship creates an atmosphere for revelation. God desires to reveal Himself to us in unlimited measure.

1.John 3:2 Beloved, now we are children of God; and it has not yet been revealed what we shall be. And we know that when He is revealed; we shall be like Him, for we will see Him as He is.

The two fiery angels carry the sound of Heaven as they blow silver trumpets, they bring heaven's witness to earth.
 The warrior angel with His sword and shield becomes a fire bolt connecting Heaven to earth as He cuts through and burns up everything that separates the two.

We can experience the manifestation of God's presence and impact of Heaven that occurs when we worship according to His own blueprint, using the adornments that are outlined in this insightful book "Heavenly Impact"

Prints available: Visual Praise Fine Art. P.O. Box 582 Social Circle, Ga. 30025

Other Great Products From Glorious Creations

Symbolic Praise Worship & Intercession
"On Earth As It Is In Heaven"
Vol. # 1

This teaching/demonstrational dvd, presents a scriptural foundation, revealing the impact created in the spiritual realm when these symbolic tools are used. Tabrets, Flags, Streamers, and Veils. 120 min. Symbolic vocabulary of movement for each instrument shown.ISBN#0-9770180-0-8

Many have used this dvd. to introduce their pastors to this type of praise and worship. We have received many reports back from teams of Intercessors from all over the country who say the Lord has showed up in so many supernatural ways since they began to worship with purpose with the instruments shown in the dvd. applying the scriptural information given in the teaching.

Symbolic Praise Worship & Intercession
"On Earth As It Is In Heaven"
Vol. #2

This DVD explores and explains the ancient history and modern application of these four worship adornments and their strategic purpose according to scripture.
Biblical references concerning these instruments reveal that our actions here on earth = reactions in heaven.

Yemenite Shofar

Prayer Shawl

Rams Horn

"World Harvest" Threshing Floor Prayer Mat

Symbolic Praise, Worship & Intercession - Vol. 2

Symbolic Praise, Worship & Intercession, Vol. 2

"On Earth as it is in Heaven"

Instructional/Demonstrational DVD. Vol. #2
ISBN# 0-9770180-1-6. www.revivalworship.com
© 2005 Jeanette Strauss Phone 517-639-4395

This DVD. explores and explains the ancient history and modern application of these four worship adornments and their strategic purpose according to scripture. Biblical references concerning these instruments reveal that our actions here on earth=reactions in heaven. 2 hours of exciting teaching/demonstration.www.revivalworship.com ISBN# 0-9770180-1-6. Glorious Creations 517-639-4395

Balm Of Gilead

Jeremiah 8:22; Is there no balm in Gilead? Is there no physician there? Why then is not the health of the daughter of my people recovered? Jeremiah 46:11: Go up to Gilead and obtain balm.

The ancient biblical Balm of Gilead is a salve made from the sap of the Balsam trees that grew in Gilead. Our Balm of Gilead is made from Balm of Gilead buds, olive oil from the Galilee region of Israel, and beeswax. All 100% natural ingredients, no perfumes added, creating a balm or salve that is smeared or rubbed upon the person seeking to be healed.

James 5:14 Is anyone among you sick? Let him call for the elders of the church and let them pray over him anointing him with oil in the name of The Lord. The word anointing here, in the Strongs Concordance is the word Aleipho, (#218) To rub, to cover over from the word Liparos, (#3045) meaning a fat or greasy substance as in ointment.
When you apply the balm and the prayers you blend the physical and the spiritual, creating an opportunity for a miracle.
www.revivalworship.com Glorious Creations 517-639-4395

166

Chrisma Consecration Anointing Oil

1.John 2:20; But ye have an unction from the Holy One, and ye know all things. The word used for unction is the Greek word #5545 : anointing: Chrisma. In Hebrew this word is Mishchah or moshchah. It is the same word used for the Old Testament consecration anointing oil used in Exodus 30:25. Moses was instructed by the Lord to create a Holy Consecration Anointing Oil made from myrrh, cinnamon, calamus, cassia, and olive oil. You will notice the oil has a strong essence, this is the Lords chosen scent, not mans. *Exodus 30:31-32 And speak to the Israelite people, as follows: This shall be a holy anointing oil sacred to Me throughout the ages. It must not be rubbed on any persons body and you must not make any like it in the same <u>proportions;</u> it is sacred, to be held sacred by you.* Proportion: This oil is prepared by the same prescription as ordained by God, but different proportions,to comply with His directions in the reproduction of this oil throughout the ages. Ref.The English translation of the Torah By the Union of American Hebrew Congregations N.Y. Copyright 1981. Ref. The Interlinear BibleHebrew/Greek/English with Strongs con-cordance numbers above each word. Sovereign Grace Publishers copyright 1976.
We put our consecration oil in purple bottles to preserve the vibrations from the pure plant matter. These vibrations are scientifically proven to be anti-bacterial and anti-viral.
www.revivalworship.com Glorious Creations 517-639-4395

Bibliography

Scripture quotes are from King James Version unless otherwise noted. All underlining of scriptures is my own emphasis.
The *Hebrew/Greek Key Study Bible. The King James Version.*
The Power New Testament. Rev.Bill Morford 2004
The Amplified Bible. Zondervan Publishing House 1965
The New American Standard Bible. The Lockman Foundation.1977
New Living Translation © 1996 Tyndale Charitable Trust
The Complete Jewish Bible. CJB.
Dake's Annotated Reference Bible. Dake Bible sales, Inc. 1963.
Webster's seventh New Collegiate Dictionary. 1961.
Scriptures marked "Torah" are from the *Torah a modern commentary* **1962, 1967.**
The Torah encompasses the first five books of the Bible, instructions from God to Israel. All Biblical translations that we now enjoy have been rooted in this book of God's instructions called the Torah. It was and still is God's original standard. When the Torah commentary uses the word Midrash it means an interpretation or expansion of a Bible text. A historical, traditional look at the scriptures, which will give us a broader picture of our subject and how it applied in Jewish tradition.

Publisher Glorious Creations © 2005 Jeanette Strauss.
1114 Robinson Rd. Quincy, Michigan 49082- 3rd. printing.
517-639-4395 www.revivalworship.com
Cover artist: Leslie Young Marks. "Painter of Truth"
www.visualpraisefineart.com cover info at the back of the book.
Graphic designer: Kristin Fisher e-mail
expressionsbykristin@yahoo.com